Beyond Human Understanding

Beyond Human Understanding

Originally Published in Spanish under the title
Más Allá del Entendimiento Humano
Lubreco Printing, Fullerton, CA 2004

English Translation by James K. McKerihan

ISBN: 1-4392-7676-5
ISBN-13: 9781439276761

Dr. Daniel Villa
www.danielvilla.com
www.impactofamiliar.com
dnvilla99@gmail.com

Library of Congress Cataloging-in-Publication Data

Villa, Daniel
Beyond Human Understanding / by Daniel Villa
p. cm.
ISBN #1-4392-6936-X
1. Christian life
BV4598

Beyond Human Understanding

Dr. Daniel Villa

Dedication

To my wife Naime, my companion and friend
To my daughter, Jessica, Lisset and Patricia
To my parents, brothers and sisters.

Contents

Special Recognition

To my wife Naime, who inspired and
encouragedme to publish these reflections.
To María Parés, Milady Gómez and James McKerihan
for their collaboration in editing this material, and to all those
who were so kind as to read it and give me their advice.

Introduction

Human convictions must be demonstrated in daily living. What we really believe becomes evident in the way we live. What we are carries more weight than what we say. If our generation is to communicate its faith, it will need not only to proclaim it but also to live that faith, and if necessary, to die for it.

We need believers who live as such in the midst of the greater and lesser challenges that daily life presents to us. People who live the gospel amid the daily tasks of the home, in their interpersonal relations, in the complex world of business, in the desperation of traffic jams; in the courts and in the jails.

How do we react when faced with suffering, betrayal, or prosperity? How do we understand a premature death? How can we deal with a "failure" without being filled with bitterness? How can we live the demands of our faith in the face of the inequalities of life and its diverse sorrows? The Christian life is a miracle, and as such is supernatural. Therefore we need a mind that is also supernatural. We need understanding that is beyond ordinary human understanding in order to live up to the standard demanded by our Teacher, and not to fail in the attempt. This is the reason that Christ places His mind within us.

This effort, which has become a book, intends to show that through the mind of Christ in believers of either sex, the Lord enables us to allow Him to live His life in us. To have "the mind of Christ" is an eminently practical matter. It is a concept that is to be applied every day and in every situation, in a continual imitation of the way Christ lived. It is a filter in the glass through which we observe human existence, blending our actions and philosophy of life with the teachings of our Lord.

The first chapter of this book explains the interpretation that we give to the biblical text of First Corinthians 2:16. In no way intending to exhaust the topic, we set forth the form and manner in which we understand and apply it, and we explain how we can obtain understanding that is beyond the human and natural. The other five chapters deal with different aspects of the Christian life, and how these situations may become more bearable when we truly assimilate the concept of having the mind of Christ, because we receive knowledge and confidence that exceed human understanding.

The author hopes that the reading of this book will be an inspirational exercise which demonstrates that the Lord Jesus Christ lives in His people, because His people live as He lived. You the reader are part of that people.

The Biblical quotations are taken from the New International Version, unless otherwise indicated.

Prologue

The author of this helpful book is well known to this writer. I have worked with him for more than eight years in planting a Hispanic church in Renton, Washington. Besides being a fellow servant of God, Pastor Villa is a warm, caring friend. He and his family are models of Christian living and dedicated pastoral service.

I read the book carefully during the process of translating it, and found it to be valuable, practical instruction for Christian living. The development of the topic "The Mind of Christ" clarifies many problem areas experienced by most believers. There is nothing surprising here, no "new revelation," but rather solid exposition illustrated by appealing anecdotes and quotations. This teaching is helpful in understanding the ways that God works in us His people. The fundamental point is that we cannot hope to understand the Lord and His working without the mind of Christ, which He imparts freely to us, but which we need to seek from Him.

This book will be helpful to anyone who reads it carefully and prayerfully, with the disposition to learn and practice its teaching.

Rev. James McKerihan

Chapter 1
THE MIND OF CHRIST

"But we have the mind of Christ."
1 Corinthians 2:16

Who could know the mind of God?
Who could equal Him in His divine wisdom?
Who ever could instruct the Lord?
Who? Who could have such understanding?

The man who can understand God does not exist
The woman that can know His mysteries does not live
It is the Father who has revealed Himself
So that mortal man may know Him as He wishes.

But how can we do His will?
Who in his heart can understand His Word?
He has given us the mind of Christ
For in giving us His Son He gave us everything.

The Holy Spirit is the good and faithful Counselor.
Jesus sent Him to us as evidence of His love.
Only He searches the deep things of God,

Dr. Daniel Villa

And helps us to understand Him to perfect our life.

So let us think with the mind of Christ
That our way of acting may be different
Let us live imitating our divine Lord
For there is no greater reward in life.

Do you have the mind of Christ? And if you do, what do you have, and how do you know that you have it? How is it useful to you? Are you using it? What changes, if any, happen in the life of the person that uses the mind of Christ? Is its use optional for us? The apostle Paul in his first letter to the Corinthians, beginning in chapter two verse six, speaks to us about knowing this "mystery," this "secret divine wisdom," referring to God's ways of working, and he tells us that the natural man, the person not led by the Holy Spirit, cannot comprehend these special forms that the Lord uses to manifest His grace and to accomplish His sovereign will.

What we understand about God through the Scriptures has been revealed to us by His Spirit, because He knows the Father, and He was sent to us so that we could understand all the marvelous things that God has given to us, for otherwise we would be incapable of comprehending them. The apostle says, "No eye has seen, no ear has heard, no mind has conceived…"[1] Yes, God has revealed such things to us who love Him. This verse is often misinterpreted, outside its natural context, applying it to the beauties which the Bible describes about the New Jerusalem. Many take delight in such thoughts, but the truth is even more glorious. It refers to the way in which God has dealt with us, the way by which it pleased Him to save us and give us the gift of eternal life. In the verse that follows the one quoted we read, "but God has revealed it to us by his Spirit."[2] How wonderful to know this!

This revelation happens because of the mind of Christ in us. We have the mind of Christ when we are guided by the Holy Spirit who dwells within us. The brain of Christ is not inserted into us, rather we are given the spiritual capacity to understand issues of faith, with the opportunity to know the Father better, and therefore to live on the spiritual plane that Jesus Christ demands of every believer. To have the mind of Christ, that is, the special capacity to understand spiritual matters, introduces us into a new dimension: the dimension of faith, of the impossible and superhuman, the dimension of God. To live without it lowers us to the level of carnal believers.

We can identify two great sources of human knowledge; one, which we will call "natural," represents the sum total of knowledge which we have acquired through study and our life experience. The other source, which we call "special," comes from what the Holy Spirit teaches us through the mind of Christ within us and the Word of God and our exercise of faith. There is no doubt that when we place ourselves in the hands of our Lord, He will use both types of knowledge, but only through the mind of Christ can we understand that we win by losing, and that "it is more blessed to give than to receive"[3]; that through dying we attain life, and that with our God, we are a majority. The Christian learns to live or to endure these paradoxes in his life by means of the mind of Christ, that is to say, with an understanding that goes beyond the merely human, the logical or rational. This is exactly what A.W. Tozer called "That Incredible Christian," and in his book by the same title he says:

> The Christian soon learns that if he wishes to be victorious as a son of heaven among earthly men, he must not follow the common norms of humanity, but exactly the opposite. To be safe, he risks his life; he loses his life to save it, and he runs the risk of losing it if he tries to save it. He goes down in order to go up. If he refuses to humble himself, he has already been humbled; but when he humbles himself, then he is exalted. He is strong when weak and weak when he feels strong. Although poor, he has the power to make others rich; and when he becomes rich, he loses his ability to enrich others. He has the most when he has given the most, and has the least when he possesses the most.[4]

Only the Holy Spirit, through the mind of Christ, can enable us to know these truths and to live as His sons and daughters; and as such, to know the Father better, being conscious of limitless power and possibilities. But in spite of the fact that our God has demonstrated His love, His grace, and His power in our favor, many times we prefer to reason things out in our weak and finite faith, rather than conducting ourselves according to the knowledge of the mind of Christ within us. This attitude was displayed by the disciples of Jesus on many occasions.

The Lord Jesus fed a multitude with five loaves of bread and two fish. Let us look more closely at this incident. John tells the story in the sixth chapter of his gospel. As we know, this is the only miracle that Jesus performed that is mentioned in all four gospels.

A crowd of about five thousand men, not counting women or children, had followed Jesus. He preached to them and taught them. When He saw that the hour was late, He asked Philip about how to get food for them all. Philip, cold and calculating, used his knowledge and said that two hundred denarius worth of bread would not be enough for the crowd, and this no doubt was true. A denarius was one day's wages of a laborer. Then Andrew approached and said, *"Here is a boy with five small barley loaves and two small fish, but how far will they go among so many?"* This also was true, logically speaking. We note that both disciples had forgotten about all the miracles that they had seen their Teacher perform. They did not consider the One before whom they stood, nor the reason He questioned them. After the amount of time that the disciples had been with the Lord (two years, more or less), they ought to have taken into consideration the accumulation of experiences they had lived with Him. It is easy from our vantage point to judge the disciples, and that is not our purpose; but the Bible indicates that they were slow to learn.[5]

It is of interest to note that John tells us that Jesus asked them about how to feed the multitude only to test them, because He knew what He would do[6]. We can defend the disciples by saying that as yet they did not have the Holy Spirit dwelling within them as we do today, and that

5

therefore they did not have the special understanding that comes with the mind of Christ in us; but that is not entirely correct. Moreover, the fact that Jesus said this to "test" them indicates that He expected a different answer. What would have been an adequate response? Let's look at two examples of the kind of answer that we think that Jesus expected. We find the first in the story that we call The Miraculous Catch of Fish. This example of a correct answer was given by Peter when the Lord asked him to cast the net into the sea to fish. Peter replied, *"Master, we've worked hard all night and haven't caught anything. But because you say so, I will let down the nets."*[7] Peter chose to act in faith, laying aside his knowledge about fishing and his failed attempts throughout the night. He could have thought and argued that he knew how to fish, and Jesus did not. That they had tried to fish that night and had nothing for their efforts; but considering who was asking him to cast the net, he decided to do it.

The second example of a correct answer we find in the Old Testament; it was given by Ezequiel when the Lord took him in the Spirit to a valley full of bones. That place looked like the scene of a bloody battle, which had left as evidence scattered human bones that the prophet said were "very dry." The Lord asked Ezequiel if he thought that those bones could live again. We don't know how long the prophet took to answer the question. Ezequiel knew, through common knowledge, that it was impossible for those bones to live again. But through his experience of faith as a priest and prophet, he also knew that God is all powerful; so he answered correctly, "O Sovereign Lord, you alone know."[8]

Yes, the mind of Christ leads us to walk no longer limited by our human understanding but by the limitless possibilities of the Lord, according to His riches in glory and His sovereign will. The Bible teaches us that we should renew our understanding, that is, change our way of thinking in order to change our way of living and so come to know the will of God.[9] Having the mind of Christ allows us to know the Father better. As we read the Scriptures, we see how He has worked, and what we can expect on that basis. The idea is not that we guess what God may do or that we can force Him into a mold. On the contrary, it means that we realize that He is Omnipotent, and that He acts by mysterious paths. It means that, faced by obstacles, we do not hesitate, knowing that if God has to violate the laws of nature in order to act, He will do so. The experience of the valiant leader Joshua is a good example. When Israel was fighting against the Amorites as night was falling, they would have become easy prey for their enemies, because they were in unknown territory. At Joshua's command made in faith, God slowed the rotation of the earth, extending the daylight and shortening the night.

But can our thoughts really coincide with God's? This will not always happen. But when it does not, we must submit our will to God's. The fact that our thoughts at a given moment are not God's does not mean that our plans and purposes are necessarily wrong. Paul and Silas wanted to preach the Word (a good thing), but the Spirit kept them from it. Their plan was not wrong, but God had other, better planes for them; and they submitted to God.

It would appear that the statement that our thoughts can coincide with God's would bring us into direct conflict with the divine declaration given by the prophet Isaiah: *"For my thoughts are not your thoughts, neither are your ways my ways," declares the Lord. "As the heavens are higher than the earth, so are my ways higher than your ways and my thoughts than your thoughts."* [10]

When analyzing Isaiah 55, we see that the entire chapter is a call to repentance, an invitation to the sinful people to return to God, who promises to pardon freely and to grant salvation and prosperity. The people were not following the path that their Lord had laid out for them. That was the situation at that moment, but it was not the norm. In fact, God's surprise in the face of the situation indicates His displeasure with it. Sin had created that great chasm between God's thoughts and those of His people. But it is not so with His sons and daughters. He has placed His trust in us and has delegated to us the task of evangelization. The Christian is led by the Holy Spirit, who knows the deep things of God. That chasm should become smaller day by day. Jesus said to His disciples, *"I no longer call you servants, because a servant does not know his master's business. Instead, I have called you friends, for everything that I learned from my Father I have made known to you."* [11] The fact that His thoughts are higher than our thoughts will always be a challenge to grow and to know God.

Through the Holy Spirit the Father has given us the mind of Christ. In this way we can walk hand in hand with our Lord. Understanding this truth will make our pilgrimage in this life easier. It will be a consolation and hope in our difficult moments. But is this really important for my Christian life? It will be decisive for our daily walk with Christ. We will understand it better if we approach the Biblical text more closely. The word in the original Greek used for "mind" in I Corinthians 2:16 is "nous." It is used 24 times in the New Testament, and is translated "mind," "understanding," and "way of thinking."[12] It is vital that every believer renew his way of thinking, because the Scripture says, *"As he thinks in his heart, so it he."*[13] This is said about a miser, but it is applicable to everyone.

We must not continue thinking according to the old patterns and values that we had before our conversion. We need a renewal of our mind in order not to go on living by our old patterns of life, but rather that we may be able to test and appreciate the good and pleasing will of God for us. Let us remember that we were enemies of God, particularly in our minds. The Bible says about us, *"Once you were alienated from God and were enemies in your minds."* [14] Satan holds the mind of the unbeliever in darkness so that he may not see nor understand the truth of the gospel. So when we come to Christ, we need to surrender our minds to the Holy Spirit for His renovation, so that we may receive the mind of Christ. Then we will begin to understand Him deeply, for we are given the capacity to understand spiritual things. It is interesting to note that Jesus had to open the understanding of the disciples that He met on the road to Emmaus so that they could understand the Scriptures.

Dr. Daniel Villa

Faced with the divisions existing in the church of Corinth, the apostle Paul makes a fervent appeal for unity; we find this in chapter one, from verse ten onward. The expression "perfectly united in mind (nous) and thought" is of special interest. What we deduce from the context is that when believers are "perfectly united," when they have the same mind and thought, conflicts are reduced to a minimum or disappear. The reason is that we see and understand spiritually and not through our carnal mind, which is selfish, stingy, self-worshiping; rather we think after the manner of God. But beware, our ideas will not always coincide. This would convert us into identical persons, without individual opinions; but the Father created us with precious individuality that we must never lose. So then, is the appeal of Paul impossible? No. It becomes authentic reality through the mind of Christ in each believer. When Paul discusses the matter of those who are weak in the faith, those who eat everything and those who abstain from certain foods, those who observe certain days and those do not, he asks each one to be convinced in his own mind. He exhorts us not to judge the brother who holds a different conviction from us. And he exclaims, *"Blessed is the man who does not condemn himself by what he approves."* [15] As we can see, we retain our individuality but we can be united through the mind of Christ within us.

The apostle Paul said to the Romans, *"Do not conform any longer to the pattern of this world, but be transformed by the renewing of your mind. Then you will be able to test and approve what God's will is—his good, pleasing and perfect will."* [16]

As we renew our mind, that is, as we change our way of thinking, our way of life will change; and we will be able to know the will of God, which is good, pleasing, and perfect.

The Bible calls us to cease to conform ourselves to this present evil world and to renew our mind. It tells us that we had a mind or understanding that was "darkened," in darkness, and we could not see the truth of the gospel. It was a mind in the pattern of the person who lives without God. We were influenced by Satan, by the world, and by our own lower instincts. In our minds we did not please God. Mentally, we were captives to diverse passions, bad habits, preconceived ideas and sinful attitudes.

Our mind was what the Scriptures call a "filthy rag." That is why we are commanded not to follow the patterns and customs that we formerly held. The Bible uses the terms "mind" and "heart" interchangeably; sometimes it defines the first as the seat of our knowledge and the second as the center of our emotions and feelings. Jesus said, *"For out of the heart come evil thoughts, murder, adultery, sexual immorality, theft, false testimony, slander."* [17] Do you see yourself there? Do you think that we can serve our Lord adequately with a mind like that? Of course not! That is why we need to renew our mind.

The command to renew our mind is given in the passive voice, which means that someone else must do it; nevertheless we must engage our full will. It is the Holy Spirit who can renew our mind, but we are the ones who allow Him to do it. The text does not say that we receive a new mind, rather that our mind is transformed. The proper word is "metamorphosis." Our mind is compared to an ugly caterpillar that can only crawl, but through the power of the Holy Spirit, it can be changed into a beautiful butterfly that conquers the flowers, flying over them. Is your mind an ugly caterpillar or a radiant butterfly?

In order for the caterpillar to become a butterfly it must submit to a process of long and difficult change. It is not easy, but it is the only way. The same thing happens to us. How does this renovation happen? It happens when we deliberately submit our mind to the control of the Holy Spirit, and we grant Him permission to break the mental molds that we have made. Over the years we have conformed to models or molds, imposed or acquired, that are determining our way of acting. We need to break those molds.

Although there can be many different molds, I will mention only a few of them:

Cultural molds.

Our culture imposes upon us certain forms and ways of thinking. We are the product of a mixture of traditions, customs, and beliefs that condition us to believe and act in a predetermined way. Everyone has this baggage, this background appropriate for the place where we were born or reared. The culture, with all its riches, has to be passed through the Biblical sieve and not the opposite. An simple example is punctuality. The Hispanic culture is not punctual.

Yes, there are people who are punctual in our culture, but the majority of us have trouble being on time. Another disagreeable inheritance in machismo. We consider women to be inferior; most men want male children.

Family molds.

Some families have traditions of infidelity, or divorce, or vices. In some cases, it is even expected that the children will act as the parent did in the same circumstances. I know a family in which the majority of the men are unfaithful. The name of that family is synonymous with infidelity. That is why in that family it is a rare thing that a man have only one wife. And what about the bad habits or improper conduct that we try to justify saying, "I inherited that from my father," or "the Rodriguez family is like that," or "we Perez are like that." All right, but what have we inherited from our heavenly Father?

Personal molds.

When a person holds on to his way of living, thinking that he cannot change, and he says, "I'm like that," "that's the way I was brought up." It is necessary to remember that in Jesus Christ we are new persons. We cannot manage our life by the values of this world. We live in a hedonistic, narcissistic society, but we must not play by its rules. We need to proclaim Jesus as Lord of our mind, and bring every thought into subjection to Christ. When one of those thoughts come that you know is not pleasing to God, say, "Lord, here is this thought. Destroy it. You are Lord of my mind."

Dr. Daniel Villa

Only a mind that is renewed and tuned in to God can discern what the Lord desires for us in every circumstance. Only a renewed mind can break the bonds of sex, drugs, pornography, gambling, or lying. Jesus places His mind in us, and we learn to think, no longer restricted to our own narrow limits, but with the values of the Kingdom. Only thus can the Holy Spirit lead us according to Christ's norms, so that we attain a new paradigm for faith and conduct.

If we attempt to live the Christian life with only an ordinary human understanding of our faith in Christ, we easily become time bombs, fair-weather sailors, or chocolate soldiers, that is to say, weak, uncommitted believers. People who do not tolerate a brother's weakness nor bear his burden, no matter how insignificant it may be. Disciples who do not understand their Teacher, and so cannot live by His standards. We need to die to ourselves, so that Christ may live His life in us, giving us His thoughts. Within us rages the battle between the desires of the flesh and those of the Spirit, which fight each other, as Paul tells us. This struggle takes place in our "command center," which is our mind. There it will be decided whether our daily decisions are made according to the flesh or according to the Spirit. Whether we will reason with our own weak mind or with the mind of Christ. The struggle is between the natural and the supernatural, between the logical and the illogical, according our finite human mind. It all depends on whether we can look where God invites us to look, so that we can run this race laying aside the roots of bitterness, the rivalries, jealousies and competition. It is a matter of living the life, or rather, dying the death that the Lord demands of us.

Chapter 2
THE METHOD OF GOD

"We know that in all things God works for the good of
those who love him."
Romans 8:28a

Do you know the story about the man and the butterfly? It goes like this:

A man found the cocoon of a butterfly and took it home to
watch when the butterfly would come out of its cocoon. One day
he noticed that there was a hole in the cocoon, and he sat for
several hours watching it. He saw that the butterfly was struggling to make the hole larger so that it could come out. The man
saw that the butterfly was straining hard, trying to push its body
through the small hole, until at one point it appeared to stop trying because it had made no progress. It seemed to have gotten
stuck. Then the kind man decided to help the butterfly, and with
a small scissors cut the side of the hole to make it larger, and so
the butterfly was able to come out of the cocoon. But when it
came out, its body was very swollen, and the wings were small
and folded up.

The man continued watching, for he expected that at any
moment the wings would unfold and grow large enough to sup-

port the body, which would contract as the swelling decreased. But nothing happened, and the butterfly could only drag itself around in circles, with its body swollen and its wings folded. It was never able to fly. What the man in his kindness and haste had not understood was that the small hole in the cocoon and the butterfly's struggle to pass through it were nature's way of forcing the fluids from its body into its wings, so that they would become large and strong, permitting the butterfly later to fly. Liberty and flight can only come through struggle. By releasing the butterfly from its struggle, the man had also deprived it of the ability to fly.

Sometimes conflicts and struggle are necessary. If God allowed us to go through life without difficulties, we would become invalids. We would not grow and become as strong as we could have become. How many times we have wanted to take the short cut to escape problems, taking the scissors and cutting through the difficulties in order to be free. We need to remember that we never receive more than we can bear and that through our struggles and our failures we are strengthened, just as gold is refined by fire.

This, doubtless, is God's method. I received this story by e-mail, and it seemed appropriate to me to illustrate the topic of this chapter. God's method for working is through surprises, in most cases, through unheard of events.

Can we come to know God better? Can we understand His attitudes and ways of working? Perhaps the answer that we most commonly meet is an emphatic No. But in the Bible we find a God who desires to be known. He has revealed Himself to us, and longs for the best possible relationship with us.

When we accept Jesus Christ as our personal Savior, we receive divine adoption as sons and daughters of God. The Holy Spirit came to dwell in our life, and gave us the mind of Christ. The Lord has made Himself known to us, how good it is to know it! The apostle Paul says that we have received *"the Spirit who is from God, that we may understand what God has freely given us."* [1] When we receive the mind of Christ, we know our Father better and we learn that our Lord works in mysterious ways. He uses methods that leave us astonished. I heard Dr. Kenn W. Opperman (a missionary of the Christian and Missionary Alliance) say that God uses people that he (Opperman) would not use, and calls people that he would not call. I agree fully with this statement. God has His methods of working, and frequently He surprises us. Through the knowledge and understanding that the mind of Christ imparts to us, we come to understand that God will work in the way and the style that He chooses, and that we cannot shut Him up in a box. To know Him is to be aware of all His resources, of His sovereign power, and of His limitless possibilities. The Bible reveals to us the multiform wisdom of God. Let's look at some examples.

Joseph, his Dream and his Reality

Genesis chapter 37 tells the story of how the problems arose between Joseph and his brothers, and how they sold him as a slave. The Bible tells us that Israel loved Joseph more than his brothers, because he was the child of his old age, and that this caused friction between the brothers. Joseph dreamed dreams on two occasions and told them to his brothers. He said to them:

Dr. Daniel Villa

> *"Listen to this dream I had: We were binding sheaves of grain out in the field when suddenly my sheaf rose and stood upright, while your sheaves gathered around mine and bowed down to it." His brothers said to him, "Do you intend to reign over us? Will you actually rule us?" And they hated him all the more because of his dream and what he had said. Then he had another dream, and he told it to his brothers. "Listen," he said, "I had another dream, and this time the sun and moon and eleven stars were bowing down to me." When he told his father as well as his brothers, his father rebuked him and said, "What is this dream you had? Will your mother and I and your brothers actually come and bow down to the ground before you?" His brothers were jealous of him, but his father kept the matter in mind.*[2]

Hatred and the root of bitterness that was in the hearts of Joseph's brothers led them to the decision to get rid of him as soon as they had an opportunity. And so as not to shed blood of the family, since they were brothers, they chose to sell him for twenty pieces of silver to the Ishmaelite traders that were passing by on their way to Egypt. We can categorize this action as one of the lowest and most despicable mentioned in the Bible. A youth about seventeen years old sold by his own brothers. Once in Egypt, the troubles and ups and downs that Joseph had to face were many; but in spite of the slander by Potiphar's wife (who accused him falsely of attempted rape), in spite of his years in prison and even of the forgetfulness of the king's cupbearer (who had promised to help him), God was with Joseph and was preparing him for the great task that He had reserved for him. Undoubtedly, God guided him to the house of Pharaoh and gave him the interpretation of the dream about the fat and gaunt cattle, which simply indicated seven years of great prosperity and good crops and seven years of famine. Thus God, through the Pharaoh, made Joseph the second ruler of all Egypt. In this position God provided food for His people Israel and also caused them to go into Egypt, where they became slaves, just as He had foretold to Abraham, Joseph's great grandfather, when God told him, *"Know for certain that your descendants will be strangers in a country not their own, and they will be enslaved and mistreated four hundred years.*[3] That prophecy was fulfilled, just as Joseph's dreams were, for his brothers came to Egypt in search of food and bowed down before him, although they did not recognize him. An act as shameful and repugnant as selling one's brother the Lord used to save lives and to accomplish all His purposes. How is this possible? God simply does it. Joseph spoke these words to his brothers: *"You intended to harm me, but God intended it for good to accomplish what is now being done, the saving of many lives."*[4] God's plans were fulfilled, using even that act rooted in hatred and bitterness. But we must emphasize that God had a plan, because did not Joseph dream his dreams even before being sold? Who gave Joseph those dreams? Who gave him the interpretation of the dreams of the Pharaoh? And who sent those years of abundance and then of famine? The answer is, The Lord did.

The certainty that Joseph had of God's care for him enabled him, even through all his suffering, not to be overcome by bitterness against his brothers, against society, or even against God Himself. Joseph knew that God would use the bad things that happened to him to bless him. This understanding comes to us today through the mind of Christ. When Joseph saw his brothers, when he had them in front of him, he had the power to take vengeance and settle accounts with them (as they feared that he would do); nevertheless, in his heart there was no resentment, because all his suffering had been God's method in order to be able to use him. Joseph said to his brothers:

> I am your brother Joseph, the one you sold into Egypt! And now, do not be distressed and do not be angry with yourselves for selling me here, because it was to save lives that God sent me ahead of you.... But God sent me ahead of you to preserve for you a remnant on earth and to save your lives by a great deliverance. So then, it was not you who sent me here, but God. He made me father to Pharaoh, lord of his entire household and ruler of all Egypt.[5]

How wonderful! Who does this? The Holy Spirit does it, giving us understanding and security beyond the normal. This allows us to see who really is our enemy. It allows us to understand clearly that our struggle is not "against flesh and blood," that is to say, not against human beings, but rather against the enemy of our soul. When we do not understand the methods of God, our life tends to be filled with sadness and anger, and roots of bitterness grow in our soul that will block our way, robbing our joy and finally leaving us in collapse along the way.

What about you? Have you been wounded and mistreated? Have your friends abandoned you? Did they betray your trust, so that you feel profoundly disillusioned? What will you do? Will you hold a grudge and seek vengeance, or will you be able to forgive, asking the Lord what He wants to teach you through all of this? Follow the example of Joseph.

How many difficulties, how much pain, what conflicts and divisions the Church of the Lord could avoid if every believer would reason using the mind of Christ! Through it we can apply to ourselves the Biblical teaching that says: *"We know that in all things God works for the good of those who love him, who have been called according to his purpose."*

Elisha and Naaman

Here we have the account of two great men, one a servant of the Most High, the other in the service of the king of Syria: Elisha, the "man of God," and the general Naaman. The Bible account tells us that Naaman, a general of the army of Syria, was a man of great valor and that he had brought glory to his people, but that this decorated Syrian hero was a leper. When Naaman learned that in Israel he could find healing, he made the journey and after some difficulties he found himself before the house where Elisha lived. Keep in mind that General Naaman traveled with a large company bringing gifts for the prophet and a letter for the king of Israel. For General Naaman this must have been a moment of suspense and tension. His leprosy was his great defect, the only dark aspect in the life of this brilliant military man. He had imagined the event, and had gone over it mentally many times; the prophet would receive him and place his hands on his blemished body, he would call to God and Naaman would be healed.[7]But things didn't happen that

21

way. The prophet did not even come out to receive him, but merely sent him by his servant this message: "Go, wash yourself seven times in the Jordan, and your flesh will be restored and you will be cleansed."[8] At first sight this appears to be an act of discourtesy by the prophet to Naaman, but God had instructed Elisha what to do. But it was too much for the proud general, who went away angry, because he did not consider that what the prophet had told him to do in order to attain his desired healing was acceptable for a man in his position. Really! Healing was not denied to him, but the general wanted God to submit to his whim, to follow his preconceived scheme; otherwise, he preferred not to be healed. It is important to note here that Naaman was not lacking in faith, rather he had predetermined the way in which the prophet should act, perhaps because of his high station. Only because of the quick intervention of his servants, who helped him see reason, Naaman finally went to the river and did as he was told, and he was healed.

As we see, God's methods or ways of acting may be very different from what we imagine. Sometimes we try to give Him suggestions about how He can do what we want Him to do, but He will always surprise us because He is an inexhaustible source of possibilities. On many occasions we too have attempted, consciously or unconsciously, to box God in to our paltry desires or methods. The mind of Christ in us will lead us to understand that He manifests Himself and acts in ways that challenge our senses and surpass our logic and understanding. Allow God to work in your life in whatever way He chooses to do so. We need only believe that God will act; His way of doing so is His affair.

The Cross as the Plan of God

Many have questioned how God could allow His Son to die on a cross. They have never accepted that this fact of history was part of the plan of God, and they present the death of Jesus as a misfortune that befell Him, due to the jealousy of the religious leaders of the time. It requires more faith to believe this that to simply accept what the Lord Himself said, that his death on the cross was God's divine plan to save us from our sins. Jesus taught, *"Just as Moses lifted up the snake in the desert, so the Son of Man must be lifted up, that everyone who believes in him may have eternal life."*[9]His own disciples, in spite of the fact that Jesus had warned them, were confused and could not understand how something like this could happen to their Teacher. This confusion was the product of their human reasoning. Cleopas, on the road to Emmaus, explained to the resurrected Christ Himself that *"the chief priests and our rulers handed him over to be sentenced to death, and they crucified him; but we had hoped that he was the one who was going to redeem Israel"*[10] In their state of mind at the moment, these disciples could not remember that He had told them that all these things would happen to Him.

Our human reasoning robs us of faith, keeping us from seeing the light that the Holy Spirit wants to give us. Although we are the sons of light, we walk in darkness, and as the poet has said, "We die of thirst before the fountain." The people of Israel did not understand that the crucifixion was the plan of God, and therefore they misunderstood it. Isaiah had foretold this when he said:

> *Surely he took up our infirmities and carried our sorrows,*
> *yet we considered him stricken by God, smitten by him,*
> *and afflicted. But he was pierced for our transgressions,*
> *he was crushed for our iniquities; the punishment that*
> *brought us peace was upon him, and by his wounds we*
> *are healed.*[11]

The people considered that crucifixion a punishment, God's rod upon Jesus. The Jews confused the cross of Christ with the judgment of God. But we know that far from being divine punishment upon one man, it was the channel of blessing for the redemption of the whole human race. When the disciples saw their resurrected Lord and He explained the Word to them again, they rejoiced in all God had ordained. The same sentiment fills our hearts when we understand the great sacrifice of Christ on the cross and the eternal love of the Father for sinners. The presence of peace and joy, no matter what the situation we must live through, is evidence that we are acting directed by the mind of Christ.

If the apostle Paul had not come to understand that his thorn in the flesh was part of God's plan for his own good (although it was difficult to accept), he would not have been able to carry forward his ministry. But when he did understand it, he said that he rejoiced in all kinds of difficulties, since he understood that his Lord knew what He was doing.[12] When we are not able to adopt an attitude like that of the apostle Paul and abandon ourselves to God, aware that He desires the best for us and that He knows what He is doing, we become bitter and get involved in friction and conflicts. But the worst part of this attitude is that the Lord cannot use us as He wishes. This understanding, which we could call wisdom, is what the mind of Christ brings us. James speaks of this wisdom when he says:

> Who is wise and understanding among you? Let him show it by his good life, by deeds done in the humility that comes from wisdom. But if you harbor bitter envy and selfish ambition in your hearts, do not boast about it or deny the truth. Such "wisdom" does not come down from heaven, but is earthly, unspiritual, of the devil. For where you have envy and selfish ambition, there you find disorder and every evil practice. But the wisdom that comes from heaven is first of all pure; then peace-loving, considerate, submissive, full of mercy and good fruit, impartial and sincere. Peacemakers who sow in peace raise a harvest of righteousness.[13]

How much we need to walk under the influence of the mind of Christ! We need to commit our minds to the power of the Holy Spirit, to go beyond our small, limited human understanding and to advance from victory to victory. We can then live the experience of the prophet Isaiah when the Lord said to him, *"Fear not, for I have redeemed you; I have summoned you by name; you are mine. When you pass through the waters, I will be with you; and when you pass through the rivers, they will not sweep over you. When you walk through the fire, you will not be burned; the flames will not set you ablaze.*[14]

Chapter 3
GOD AND PROTECTION

"God is our refuge and strength, an ever-preset help in trouble. Therefore we will not fear, though the earth give way and the mountains fall into the heart of the sea."
Psalm 46:12

Have you heard about James? Yes, James? He was an extraordinary man. A fisherman by trade, he lived in one of the most fabulous epochs of human history. One morning while he was repairing the fishing nets with his father Zebedee and his brother John, Jesus of Nazareth called him and his brother and joined them with His small group of disciples, to later change them into the apostles sent to evangelize the world in the name of their Teacher. When Jesus called them, He gave them the descriptive name "Boanerges, Sons of Thunder."James, his brother John, and Peter formed what is known as Jesus' small circle of friendship. We remember that He later had a total of seventy disciples, whom He sent out to preach two by two. Within the seventy He had a smaller group, the twelve, with whom He spent more time and really shared His life with them, teaching them and modeling for them His principles of faith. But even within the twelve was this small, intimate group.

They were James, his brother John, and Peter. These were called by Jesus to accompany Him in key, sensitive moments of His ministry. They were with Him on the extraordinary occasion of His Transfiguration, as well as during His painful struggle in Gethsemane. Moreover, they were the only ones who remained with the Teacher when they prayed for the resurrection of the daughter of Jairus. On each one of these events in the life of the Savior, James was present; he was an inseparable friend.

These two brothers were the protagonists in two incidents that are worth mentioning. The first happened when Jesus and His disciples were on their way to Jerusalem and tried to find lodging in a city of the Samaritans, but the inhabitants refused to receive them. James and John were angered by the attitude of the residents of that town and said to the Teacher, *"Lord, do you want us to call fire down from heaven to destroy them?"*[2] Jesus rebuked them and did not allow them to do what they had requested. But such was the zeal and the love of these men for the Messiah.

The second occasion when they were also rebuked happened because of the daring of these brothers, apparently in the company of their mother, in requesting from the Lord to occupy the most important places at His side on the heavenly throne. No matter how reproachable both these incidents may be, they show clearly, as already commented, the love, faith, and unfaltering trust of these men in every promise of their Teacher.

We may ask ourselves, therefore, James being what he was, with such a firm commitment and complete surrender, why the Lord allowed him to die so early in the history of the Church. We may answer that precisely for this reason Jesus allowed him to drink from His cup, because he was prepared and willing to do so. James, together with Stephen, becomes one of the first martyrs of the Church. Peter and James were arrested by Herod. The former was liberated miraculously, but the latter was sacrificed. The Lord allowed Peter to live for Him, while James was allowed to die for Him. In both cases, God's protection was present. In both His name was glorified. Can we understand this?

The confidence of the psalmist David is outstanding when he proclaims that the Lord is his refuge and strength, as we quoted at the beginning of this chapter. Under the protection of God he feels confident and completely secure. He does not fear tribulation or bad times, whether they come from people or nature. What circumstances cause fear to you? Frequently loneliness, darkness, the close presence of an unknown person, or some phenomenon of nature (earthquake, hurricane, etc.) are causes of our fears. To these we must add the painful presence of anxiety, which although it also implies fear, is internal. It is fear without a justifying cause.[3] We feel protected if we have company, if we are in a "safe" house, if we have a watch dog, or if we have some weapon to defend ourselves. These feelings are very human. But when we understand that we belong to God and that He is our refuge, our attitude and our feelings toward the circumstances mentioned ought to change.

Dr. Daniel Villa

There is a legend about an interesting competition for painters that goes like this:

> A competition was announced for painters on the topic of "Peace." A number of paintings were entered, one of a peaceful morning, another of a silent sunset, and other similar works. But the prize was awarded to a picture that showed a thunderous cataract that plunged over a rocky cliff, producing thick clouds of foam and mist. But on the branch of a tree that extended over the boiling cauldron a robin had built its nest and was singing merrily. Certainly, the best concept of peace is that which can be obtained and enjoyed, not in favorable circumstances, but in the midst of noise and tempest. The robin was sitting on a branch that had its roots in the rock and that extended over the boiling mist of the cataract. In that high place nothing could harm it. So should be the peace of those who have put their trust in the God of heaven.[4]

Do we believers have such confidence? It is really a contradiction to ask whether a "believer" has confidence. When the Holy Spirit gives us the mind of Christ, He makes us understand that we can turn over all anxiety and care to Jesus, and that whatever may happen, our Lord will know how to use it in some way to bless us. In Psalm 127:1 the psalmist says, *"Unless the Lord watches over the city, the watchmen stand guard in vain."*

It does not matter that a powerful army is camped near us, whether to defend us or to attack us. God will work His will regarding us. (That divine will may not necessarily agree with our plans or desires.) We have an example in the deliverance of Peter from Herod's jail, in spite of the watching guard.[5] Also in the confidence of the prophet Elisha, when he told his frightened servant not to be afraid of the Syrian army that was besieging them. *"Those who are with us are more than those who are with them,"*[6] he said, referring to the army of angels that was surrounding that place. King David had this same confidence when he said in Psalm 27:3, *"Though an army besiege me, my heart will not fear; though war break out against me, even then will I be confident."*

Now, what makes us feel more secure? To have an army ready to defend us, or to be completely alone, pursued by that same army, fortified only with the knowledge that the Lord is protecting us? With the strengthening that the mind of Christ brings us, we will exchange the army for the protection of the Lord.

The shepherd David knew that in the same way that he protected and provided for his sheep, God would protect and provide for him, and he wrote:

> The Lord is my shepherd, I shall not be in want. He makes me lie down in green pastures, he leads me beside quiet waters, he restores my soul. He guides me in paths of righteousness for his name's sake. Even though I walk through the valley of the shadow of death, I will fear no evil, for you are with me; your rod and your staff, they comfort me.[7]

Dr. Daniel Villa

David's words and actions were in agreement, for in his moments of anguish when pursued by King Saul, David trusted more in the will and the plans of God for his life than in his sword. Our human concept of trust in God is very limited, and in most cases we trust to the Lord only those things that we cannot do ourselves. Let's try to illustrate like this: we parents pray for protection for our children most urgently when they are not with us, or when for some reason we cannot help them. We pray, "Oh, Lord, protect my son, because that road he is on is dangerous," or "Help him to do well on his exam," etc. While our child is out of the house, our prayers are incessant. But as soon as he gets home, our prayers cease, because he is within reach. In our subconscious mind we have the idea that we can protect him. There is nothing wrong with this attitude, except that the intensity of our intercession should be always the same, because it is God who really must protect them, far beyond what we can do. It is our duty to intercede constantly for our children, whether they are close to us or not.

Some years ago we left our home for five days to attend the annual conference of our denomination. We lived in a small house with very little protection. My wife and I were newly married and our few possessions were in that remote, isolated house. During the entire conference I was continually praying that the Lord would protect the house. Some nights I woke up frightened, having dreamed that someone had entered the house to rob. Then I would insist in my prayers, "God, protect our house from thieves." When we returned home one Sunday afternoon, everything was as we had left it. We thanked the Father for this. From then on our prayers for God's care over the house decreased, and moreover, my prayers were more relaxed, more calm, perhaps because we were there, and no one would dare to break in under those circumstances. Nevertheless, the night of the following Tuesday, when we were there, someone came in while we were sleeping and took everything, even what was in the refrigerator! How ironic! They stole from us, as the saying goes, "right from under our noses." No doubt about it, God was teaching us a great lesson: I am always your protector. It was a lesson we learned.

Now, when we exercise the mind of Christ, we understand that His protection is not necessarily a blanket protection against all harm; rather, it is the certainty that the Lord will do the best for my life, according to His purpose, although this may not be to our entire satisfaction and pleasure. Let's look at God's promise to the prophet Jeremiah:

> "Do not be afraid of them, for I am with you and will rescue you," declares the Lord. "Today I have made you a fortified city, an iron pillar and a bronze wall to stand against the whole land—against the kings of Judah, its officials, its priests and the people of the land. They will fight against you but will not overcome you, for I am with you and will rescue you," declares the Lord.[8]

The promises that the Lord made to Jeremiah were faithful, and He kept them even in difficult days; but in our weak human mind, we think that having received a declaration like the one he received, Jeremiah would not suffer the poverty and sadness that he had to face, as well as suffering the rejection of his own family and the people to whom he ministered. It is commonly believed that if a person is called to minister to a certain group, he needs to be popular and loved by them, as proof of God's backing, but it was not so with Jeremiah. Another cause of pain was to see his people go into captivity in a foreign land, all because of the hardness of their hearts. Christian tradition says that Jeremiah was stoned to death in Tahpanhes, Egypt, by the Jews, his beloved people. Did God protect him? Totally. Jeremiah successfully completed the work God had committed to him. If we look at him apart from the mind of Christ, we will doubt God's divine protection and even more his triumph.

God protects us, yes, He does; but when we have the mind of Christ we can accept the death of so many Christians in the Roman circus. We accept the death of Hernando Hernández, a young Colombian leader who served the Lord with great dedication. Hernando had a beautiful ministry to university students when he died in violent automobile accident. And what shall we say about the death of the tragic and inspiring death of the five North American missionaries at the hands of the Auca tribe in the jungle of Ecuador? Those missionaries were killed while they were attempting to take the gospel to that tribe. They were: Nate Saint (31 years old), Roger Youderian (31), Jim Elliot (28), Edward MacCully (28), and Pete Fleming (27).[9] Some time later, Elisabeth Elliot, the widow of Jim Elliot, and other relatives of the martyrs, went to work among the Aucas, the same tribe that killed their family members. There they met several of those who participated in the killing, and they told them about God's love for every individual. After those deaths, the Christian world focused its eyes, its prayers, and its efforts to reach the inhabitants of that remote region, many of whom today have found salvation in Jesus Christ.

God protects us, we are His special people, His precious treasure. We are safe in His hands; we fear nothing, not even death, because at any given moment it may be part of God's plan for some of His dear children. Let us always remember that whatever happens to us God will use in some way to fulfill His purposes and plans, and He will turn any evil that touches us into a wholesome, enriching experience. Sadly, the concept of protection that many Western believers have is Hollywood style protection. Armed with God's promises, we think that we are the heroes of one of those movies where nothing can happen to the lead actor, who overcomes everything, surpasses his objectives and exterminates his enemies without suffering a scratch, and doesn't even lose his hat!

Jesus bought us through His vicarious sacrifice; we belong to Him and are satisfied with that. Sometimes He permits us to drink from His cup and other times He does not. Some live to tell their experiences, while others are called to His presence. Whether we live or die, we are the Lord's, who always shows us His favor.

To the question, Can or should a good Christian suffer? We can reply with another question: Who was the greatest Christian who ever lived? If the answer is Jesus

Dr. Daniel Villa

Christ, which it is, we ask ourselves again, Did He suffer? Did He say that we would suffer? Did He or did He not invite us to take up His cross? What we have said here does not mean that we understand the cause or source of all suffering and that we always have an answer or explanation for it. Truly, I have known inexplicable, disconcerting situations, but the main point here is not our understanding of every case, which would amount to having the answer to the question, Why, Lord? I believe that even though God would sit down beside us and would explain the why of many of our troubles, not even then would we fully understand. The Word of God tells us that there are things that we will understand only when we are with the Lord. What is useful to us and comforts us is to know that we are loved and protected by Him. It is to trust that He sustains us, always remembering that this does not mean that nothing "bad" will happen to us; rather, that the Lord is with us and even that unwanted thing that may happen, He will know how to transform into a blessing. In stead of asking, Why? we should ask, What for, Lord? What do you want me to learn? What do you want to teach me?

You may look back at your past and remember your saddest, most difficult moments, or you may contemplate the storm that you are presently going through. God is by your side; He understands you and protects you, and from the ashes of your pain He will lift you up and heal you. As the poem about the footprints says, He carries us in His arms. Strange to say, few experiences enrich our lives more than the lessons born in pain. The psalmist David in Psalm 23 not only mentions the still waters and green pastures, but he also speaks of the valley of affliction. For in the Christian life we have moments of peace and tranquility but also of pain and deep sorrow. But in both of these Jesus is our Shepherd and He never leaves us.

As we cross the valley of affliction, a special, rare sediment is deposited upon the earth of our existence which allows to flower in our lives a variety of roses that adorn only the lives of those who have learned to grow in the midst of their afflictions. Someone expressed it this way:

> I walked a mile with Pleasure, and she talked with me the whole time, but when we separated, she had not said anything of importance to me. I walked a mile with Pain, and not a word passed between us, but oh, how much I learned from her when we shared our path![10]

The wives, children, and other family members of the five martyrs of the faith who gave up their lives to reach the Aucas, found comfort in the words that they found in Jim Elliot's diary, with which we conclude this chapter.

> I walked out to the hill just now. It is exalting, delicious, to stand embraced by the shadows of a friendly tree with the wind tugging at your coattail and the heavens hailing your heart, to gaze and glory and give oneself again to God—what more could a man ask? Oh, the fullness, pleasure, sheer excitement of knowing God on earth! I care not if I never raise my voice again for Him, if only I may love Him, please Him. Mayhap in mercy He shall give me a host of children that I may lead them through the vast star

fields to explore His delicacies whose finger ends set the to burning. But if not, if only I may see Him, touch His garments, and smile into His eyes—ah, then, not stars nor children shall matter, only Himself. O Jesus, Master and Center and End of all, how long before that Glory is thine which has so long waited Thee? Now there is no thought of Thee among men; then there shall be thought for nothing else. Now other men are praised; then none shall care for any other's merits. Hasten, hasten, Glory of Heaven, take Thy crown, subdue Thy Kingdom, enthrall Thy creatures.[11]

Chapter 4
GOD AND STRENGTH

"The Lord is my light and my salvation—whom shall I fear?
The Lord is the stronghold of my life—of whom shall I be
afraid?"
Psalm 27:1

When we say that someone or something is our strength, we are saying that from that source we obtain strength and vigor to face the challenges and struggles of life, or that it is our support in facing a severe crisis. In moments of great anguish in his life, David expressed that God and God alone was the light, the salvation and the strength of his life. For King David, the source of his confidence and hope was not in his army or his dexterity with weapons, but rather in the Lord.

Who or what is your strength? What is the divine concept of strength that the Scriptures reveal to us? Is it similar to our concept? Regarding this concept, as well as any other we may have, we need to ask ourselves and seek to discover how God sees it, and what He says about it. In the light of the Word of God we can define moral strength as strength in weakness. This paradox is only understandable, and hence useful, by means of the mind of Christ in us. Without that capacity we would never be able to understand the apostle Paul when he says, *"When I am weak, then I am strong."*[1] We will illustrate this Biblical truth with some examples.

David and Goliath

This well-known story shows us clearly what a person with the mind of Christ is capable of doing for God. Try to imagine the scene: the huge, swaggering Goliath from a nearby hill was challenging the frightened Israelites, who were listening to him from the other side of the valley without daring to confront the fearsome Philistine. Goliath was a seasoned warrior over nine feet tall. The Bible describes his weapons: *"He had a bronze helmet on his head and wore a coat of scale armor of bronze weighing five thousand shekels; on his legs he wore bronze greaves, and a bronze javelin was slung on his back. His spear shaft was like a weaver's rod, and its iron point weighed six hundred shekels."*[2]

Goliath appeared to be an invincible warrior. His safety and strength were based in himself, in his skill, strength, and size; and on him were pinned the hopes of the Philistines. On the other side was David, a simple shepherd, with no military experience and who was not even part of the army of Israel. David was there because he had been sent by his father to visit his brothers who were in military service. David heard the insults that Goliath was spouting and how he was challenging the Israelites, asking for someone to dare to fight to the death with him. The son of Jesse reacted with anger and offered to fight the Philistine. King Saul told him that he could not fight Goliath because he was a "boy," that is, very young and inexperienced. And that was true. The logical reasoning of Saul told him that this "boy" could not successfully face a mammoth of a man like Goliath. But David was not looking at himself. He knew that he was incapable of facing the imposing enemy. He was not able, but his Lord was! His strength lay in his confidence that Almighty God would protect him; and just as he had faced the wild animals that attacked his flock, so he was prepared to fight the gigantic Philistine, because the Lord was his strength. When he faced Goliath, David said to him:

> You come against me with sword and spear and javelin, but I come against you in the name of the Lord Almighty, the God of the armies of Israel, whom you have defied.[3]

Here we see strength in weakness. Once again David declares that his strength is in God. He did not go forth relying on his experience in hunting, nor on his skill with the sling, but on the Lord. And with this faith he armed himself with five smooth stones, his sling, and his firm confidence in God. I heard Dr. J Vernon McGee say that David took five stones, not in case he missed the giant, but rather because Goliath had four brothers like himself. Could David's confidence have been that strong? Yes, it was. The little shepherd was convinced that one stone was enough to knock down his opponent, because it was not the stone, the sling, nor his skill, but God who would do the miracle. And if four more giants appeared, he had a stone for each one of them.

Dr. Daniel Villa

When we look at this scene through the mind of Christ, we lose our human concept of strength, and we see that the true giant was the simple shepherd of Bethlehem, not the Philistine champion, who had the misfortune of challenging "the army of the living God."

The mind of Christ permits us to have a clear, complete vision of each circumstance that we live, for our eyes give us only part of the picture. Our battle, although it is reflected in this physical world, is eminently spiritual; therefore our strength must be spiritual. The understanding that David had of God (the mind of Christ in us) allowed him to see things that were hidden to others. Take for example the words of Goliath: *"Am I not a Philistine, and are you not the servants of Saul?"*[4] This was true; the Israelites were servants of Saul. That was how far the vision or knowledge of Goliath went, and apparently, of the whole army of Israel as well. But how did David see things? He said, "*Who is this uncircumcised Philistine that he should defy the armies of the living God?*"[5] David saw them as "servants of the living God." Therefore the insults were not directed against Saul only but against God Himself, and so he could expect the quick, exemplary response from the Lord. Later, Saul tried to dress David in all the armor that he had; but David could barely walk in it and requested not to use it. He knew that what was important was not his weapons, but the presence and help of God. He said this to Goliath, *"All those gathered here will know that it is not by sword or spear that the Lord saves, for the battle is the Lord's."*[6]

All of God's power was there from the beginning, ready to be manifested, but what was needed was someone who could see it, could understand it and appropriate it; and this is possible only through the understanding which the Lord gives us. This story of David and Goliath is not similar to the fables of the hare and the tortoise or the eagle and the snail, in which the weak through their own effort and overcoming many difficulties achieve their goal and defeat those who appear to be invincible. No, David did not go into battle confiding in his own will power or in his destiny or good luck; David knew God and understood that for God all things are possible. Through the mind of Christ we can look at our weakness, proclaim the Lord as our strength, and advance with confidence, for in His hands we are safe.

Gideon and his Army

Here is another interesting case in which we can define strength as strength in weakness. In contrast to David, who had no weapons of war, Gideon, aware of God's call, organized an entire army and could have been tempted by the human concept of strength. It is necessary to state that Gideon's story happened about 130 years before David's. We want to contrast the lack resources in David's case with the abundance that Gideon had, and how God works in each case. We remember that Israel had no king in those days. After Joshua died, the people were left without a national leader to guide them, which produced anarchy and disunion among the people. There was disobedience to God's commands, and Israel was subjugated to the power of the neighboring peoples because of her sins. From time to time, when the people would repent, the Lord would send leaders who were known as "judges," who would free them from their slavery, and the people would again walk in obedience; but when the judges died, the people fell back to their sinful ways.

For seven years Israel had been delivered into the hands of the people of Midian. When they cried out to God because of the Midianites, the Lord raised up Gideon to liberate them. This man, convinced that the Lord would deliver the Midianites into his hands, and manifesting his gifts as a leader and military strategist, called the people together and organized them into an army of 32,000 men to face the enemy. This was based on logical reasoning; the bigger and more powerful the army, the easier would be the victory. However, this was not the plan of God. Let's look at what the Bible says in Judges 2:2-7:

> The Lord said to Gideon, "You have too many men for me to deliver Midian into their hands. In order that Israel may not boast against me that her own strength has saved her, announce now to the people, 'Anyone who trembles with fear may turn back and leave Mount Gilead.'" So twenty-two thousand men left, while ten thousand remained. But the Lord said to Gideon, "There are still too many men. Take them down to the water, and I will sift them for you there. If I say, 'This one shall go with you,' he shall go; but if I say, 'This one shall not go with you,' he shall not go." So Gideon took the men down to the water. There the Lord told him, "Separate those who lap the water with their tongues like a dog from those

*who kneel down to drink." Three hundred men lapped
with their hands to their mouths. All the rest got down on
their knees to drink. The Lord said to Gideon, "With the
three hundred men that lapped I will save you and give
the Midianites into your hands. Let all the other men go,
each to his own place."*

God did not need that large army to do His will. He
used less that one per cent of them, and gave them the
victory over Midian. Gideon learned a new concept of
strength—"strength in weakness." That is, divine power
in human weakness, when the Lord is our strength. Without doubt Gideon became a different man when he understood this concept, but do we understand it? Through the
mind of Christ we can understand that the Lord is our only
strength. When the psalmist remembered and sang of the
wonders of the Lord throughout the history of Israel, he
said, *"It was not by their sword that they won the land, nor did
their arm bring them victory; it was your right hand, your arm,
and the light of your face, for you loved them."*[7] We remember
the hymn "Victory through Grace" and its chorus, which
says, "Not to the strong is the battle, Not to the swift is
the race, Yet to the true and the faithful Victory is promised
through grace."[8]

The Apostle Paul and his Ministry

Up to now we have looked at cases of warfare where
a physical enemy had to be faced, and the Lord showed His
strength and power overcoming the enemy in the face of
apparent weakness (real human weakness). The case of the
apostle is completely different. Jesus called him from his

position of a zealous persecutor of the church, transformed his life and made him an apostle of the gospel, although he had not been with the Teacher like the twelve disciples who had always accompanied Him. Paul declared that he left everything that was to his advantage, considering it loss (rubbish) for the love of Christ.[9] For the love of his Teacher, he forsook even his prestigious position as a Pharisee in the heart of Jewish society. But in exchange, the apostle Paul received the grand commission of evangelizing the Gentiles. In truth, his only possession came to be Christ and the ministry he had received. Then Paul's motive for living became his apostolic ministry. It is logical to suppose that he would exert himself to his full capacity in his calling. And so he besought God to remove a thorn in his flesh, that is, a physical affliction that the apostle never identified. This is doubtless a deliberate part of God's purpose for us (some think it was a physical infirmity,[10] others, that it was a person that continually annoyed him[11]). But what is completely clear is that God had a purpose in not answering Paul's prayers for the removal of the thorn. Possibly He intended that the extraordinary experiences of the apostle would not become a stumbling block to him, allowing him to become puffed up, thinking that he was accomplishing everything through his own strength. Because of the magnitude of his calling, Paul needed to be vigorous, healthy, and free. He did not need additional enemies to block his path. For this reason he prayed three times to be freed from the "thorn" that was causing him embarrassment, suffering, and shame. But the Lord showed the apostle that his strength was not in his health, nor in his resources or opportunities, and not even in his former relationships, rather that to fulfill the ministry committed to him, God's grace would be sufficient. The Lord said to him, *"My grace is sufficient for you, for my power is made perfect in weakness."*[12] Paul learned, through the mind of Christ, that he could do more with the grace of God than with his health; that God's love was worth more to him than money or possessions; that God's grace would be more useful to him for his ministry than anything that would help him to feel secure and greater freedom. When he understood this, the apostle exclaimed:

> *Therefore I will boast all the more gladly about my weaknesses, so that Christ's power may rest on me. That is why, for Christ's sake, I delight in weaknesses, in insults, in hardships, in persecutions, in difficulties. For when I am weak, then I am strong.*[13]

The only thing Paul needed was the love of God, for when he felt weak, all the power of the Lord could act upon him, because His power is manifested in our inadequacy. This is strength in weakness. It demands a total surrender on our part: a complete abandonment into the hands of God. It does not happen through our means or possibilities; He is our strength. Only by reasoning with the mind of Christ does this become possible.

Lloyd J. Ogilvie tells of his experience regarding this in his book *Falling into Greatness:*

> Falling into greatness? The words seem contradictory, but only at first. Allow me to explain. What I've learned about falling successfully is that in times of inadequacy, I experience how great the Lord is. In

times of ease or triumph I can readily acknowledge His glory with gratitude; but when life goes bump, I realize the greatness of His gracious heart. There are aspects of the Lord's nature we never experience until we are forced to face our inadequacy, insufficiency, and inability.[14]

So it is. We would never know divine healing if we never became sick. We will never experience God as our Provider if all our needs are met. Our experience of the Lord as our Provider may mean very different things, depending on the part of the world where we live; but the truth is the same: our heavenly Father supplies our needs when we have them.

Let's think for a moment about Christ on the cross. Those who put Him there thought that they had put an end to the threat represented by the new movement. His own disciples thought that everything had ended. But that death was a fountain of life; what appeared to be defeat was in reality the greatest victory ever won. In the midst of the dense darkness of the moment, the Light of the World was illuminating all of humanity. In Revelation we are told that John wept, because no one in heaven or on earth or under the earth was found worthy to break the seals and open the book. But one of the elders said to him, *"Do not weep! See, the Lion of the tribe of Judah, the Root of David, has triumphed. He is able to open the scroll and its seven seals."*[15] We are told that John immediately looked, but what did he expect to see? He had been told that "the Lion of the tribe of Judah" was there and had triumphed. Would it not be logical for him to expect to see a lion in all its ferocity and majesty? But when he looked, the Scripture tells us that he said, "I saw a Lamb, looking as if it had been slain, standing...."[16] This is the concept of strength that we see in God. That "Lion of the tribe of Judah" was nothing more than a Lamb that appeared to have been sacrificed, helpless and dead. But precisely there, in the sacrifice of the Lamb, was the strength of the Lion. How beautiful! The mind of Christ enables us to understand it. We need to live under the influence of the mind of Christ in order to understand and apply to our faith pilgrimage the divine concept of strength.

Leighton Ford, in his book *The Christian Persuader,* speaking of the preaching of the gospel, says:

> What would the critics have said if they had seen that Jewish carpenter preaching from a boat and hanging from a cross? Would they have guessed that He, and not the Roman legions, would be the "hinge of history"? Can you imagine how contemptuously they would have dismissed Paul's preaching in Athens? Could they have guessed that the message he preached would smash paganism and turn the Parthenon itself into a Christian church for centuries to come? Which event would they have picked as most relevant in the early years of the fifth century: Alaric's sacking of the city of Rome in 410, or Augustine's writing of *The City of God* in 413? Yet is was the bishop's book, not the barbarian's bands, that controlled the Middle Ages. Suppose they had lived in eighteenth-century England while revolution was brewing across the Channel and threatening in their own land, and had heard John Wesley preaching in a field. They would have cried, "Come down to earth!

> Problems enough here. Forget heaven. Be relevant."
> But Lecky has said that the Wesleyan revival saved
> England from the French Revolution.[17]

Oh, brothers and sisters, let us die to ourselves and let us live for our Lord! Let us walk, no longer trusting in our strength and possibilities, in our abilities and relationships, but rather in His unlimited resources, which are greater and better than ours. May our security not rest in our finances or position, nor the size of the congregation to which we minister, nor our bank account. Let us avoid placing our confidence in any temporal possibility, whether a person or a thing. May Christ place His mind within us so that we may see Him as our only strength.

Let us conclude with this interesting story of a mountain climber who was possessed by the ambition to climb Mt. Aconcagua, and prepared diligently for years for this attempt. He decided to do it alone, since he did not wish to share that moment of glory with anyone. He began to climb, full of enthusiasm and propelled by a strange anxiety to reach his goal. When night began to fall, he did not prepare to camp, but instead continued on in order to reach the peak as soon as possible. The night fell extremely dark over the mountain height, and he could see absolutely nothing. Everything was black, visibility zero, no moon, and the stars blacked out by clouds. As he climbed a cliff, only one hundred meters from the peak, he slipped and plummeted through the air. He was falling at dizzying speed, and could see only darker forms that passed him in the blackness, with the terrifying feeling of being sucked down by gravity. As he fell, thinking that he would die, through his mind raced all the happy and less happy moments of his life. Suddenly he felt a jerk so strong that it almost pulled him in half. Like all experienced alpinists, he had anchored security stakes and attached a long line to his waist. As he dangled in the air, suspended by his line, all he could do was cry, "God, help me!" Suddenly, he heard a deep, solemn voice saying, "What do you want me to do, my son?" "Save me, oh God!" "Do you really believe that I can save you?" "Of course, Lord," the man replied. "Then cut the cord that is holding you up." There was a moment of silence, and the man clung more tightly to the line. The following day a rescue crew told the tale of an alpinist who was found, frozen to death, clinging with both hands to a rope, only six feet above the ground. What about you, how much do you trust in your rope? Why don't you let it go? It is necessary to learn to trust in God and not in ourselves, nor in our "ropes." Could it be that we are too attached, in one way or another, to some rope? Who or what really is your strength? [18]

Chapter 5
GOD AND GREATNESS

"Great is the Lord and most worthy of praise;
his greatness no one can fathom."
Psalm 145:3

In this chapter we wish to point out that God alone is truly great and powerful. No other power, whether human or angelic, can be compared to Him, or lies outside His authority. Only the person whom the Lord considers great is truly great, no matter what the appearances may be. True honor and genuine greatness come from our supreme King and Lord. ¿How can these be obtained? Come with me.

God is Great

When God revealed Himself to Abraham, He made Himself known as "El Shaddai" which means the one "possessing all power in heaven and on earth."[1] The psalmist David sings in Psalm 19 about the manifestation of the divine glory throughout all creation. He says, "The heavens declare the glory of God; the skies proclaim the work of his hands." All nature, by its thousands of colors, by the heights of the mountains, by the depths of the precipices, by the songs of the birds and the immensity of the sea, by sunsets and starry skies, by mischievous rains and soft breezes, by all of these it speaks to us of "El Shaddai," our great and powerful Lord. The inspired hymnologist sang:

> O Lord my God! When I in awesome wonder consider all the worlds Thy hands have made, I see the stars, I hear the rolling thunder, Thy power throughout the universe displayed. When through the woods and forest glades I wander and hear the birds sing sweetly in the trees; When I look down from lofty mountain grandeur and hear the brook and feel the gentle breeze. Then sings my soul, my Savior God, to Thee. How great Thou art, how great Thou art![2]

The word "magnificence" is a synonym for "greatness," and so we read in Psalm 93:1, *"The Lord reigns, he is robed in majesty; the Lord is robed in majesty and is armed with strength."* Our God covers Himself with greatness and majesty. The Bible tells us, *"God comes in awesome majesty. The Almighty is beyond our reach."* The English theologian J.I. Packer expresses it this way: "The word 'majesty', when applied to God, is always a declaration of His greatness and an invitation to worship."[3] Packer also points out how significant it is that the author of the Book of Hebrews used the term "the Majesty" in place of the word God.[4] Speaking about our Lord Jesus Christ, Hebrews 1:3 and 8:1 say, *"After he had provided purification for sins, he sat down at the right hand of the Majesty in heaven."*

The greatness of the Lord is also shown in that He is the God of gods. When Moses told his father-in-law all that the Lord had done for him and for the people, Jethro exclaimed, *"Now I know that the Lord is greater than all other gods,"*[5] But even before that occasion, when Israel crossed the Red Sea on dry land she sang, *"Who among the gods is like you, O Lord? Who is like you—majestic in holiness…?"*[6] The fact is that there is no god comparable to our God. He, and He alone, is great and powerful. We do not mean to say that other gods exist, for only the Lord is God. But when Israel compared her Lord and God with the gods of the neighboring peoples, when she meditated on His excellent deeds, His exploits and mighty acts, she exclaimed, "Who among the gods is like you, O Lord?" But how great is our God? The Lord is immeasurable; that is to say, He cannot be measured. There is no one or nothing with which He can be compared. The prophet Isaiah illustrated this truth for us when he asked, *"Who has measured the waters in the hollow of his hand, or with the breadth of his hand marked off the heavens? Who has held the dust of the earth in a basket, or weighed the mountains on the scales and the hills in a balance?"*[7]

The first question we are asked is, who measured the waters in the hollow of his hand? The obvious answer is that our God did this. But is it possible to do such a thing? When you press your fingers together and form a hollow in your palm, how much water can it hold? What quantity of water are we talking about? Let's see. Some people maintain that our planet should be called Ocean and not Earth, since the oceans cover two thirds of the surface of our world. 71% of the surface of the earth is water, that is, about 362 million square kilometers. The seas and oceans contain 97% of the water of the planet.[8] The deepest parts of the ocean floor are the trenches, where the ocean is about 11,000 meters deep.[9] The Bible tells us that our God took that enormous quantity of water and held it in the hollow of His hand. Hallelujah! Can this Lord protect you? Yes, He can do it. If you are ever upon the high seas, think that you are in the hollow of His hand! We can join our voices with the psalmist when he sings in Psalm 93:3-4:

> *The seas have lifted up, O Lord, the seas have lifted up their voice; the seas have lifted up their pounding waves. Mightier than the thunder of the great waters, mightier than the breakers of the sea—the Lord on high is mighty.*

A second question that we take from the text is, who gathered together the dust of the earth and weighed the mountains and hills? Again, the answer is, the Lord did it. This is our incomparable God. Who but He could gather together the highest mountain peaks and hills of the earth? J.H. Barrows once said, *"The mountain ranges are letters in high relief upon which we, blind children, place our fingers in order to read the name of God."*[10] We are awed by the immense height of the lofty mountains that appear to us to touch the sky. The Orizaba Peak in Mexico, 5,700 meters high. Chimborazo (Ecuador), 6,267 meters. Aconcagua (Argentina), 6,960 meters. Mount Communism, 7,495 meters (Tadjikistan, in the former Soviet Union). The K-2 Peak (also known as Godwin Austen, 8,611 meters (Indo-Pakistani border). And Mount Everest (the Himalayas, on the Nepal-Chinese border), the highest point on earth, with its 8,848 meters.[11] The Bible tells us that God gathered together the dust of the earth and weighed the mountains in a balance. That is how great He is. The next time you are on a mountain, think that you are in the hand of God!

The third question we find is, who measured the heavens with the breadth of his hand? That is to say, the palm of His hand was all the Lord needed to measure the entire universe. Planet Earth is located in the solar system, which consists of nine planets (four of them several times larger than Earth), plus natural satellites, asteroids, comets, meteoroids, and interplanetary dust. The sun is the only star in the system.[12] The distance between the earth and the sun is about 149,598,000 kilometers. This distance has been used as a measurement, and it is called an astronomical unit (a.u.), which, as we have said, is equal to the distance from the earth to the sun. Pluto, the planet farthest from the sun, is 39.785 a.u. distant.[13] Is it possible to imagine this distance?

Now we must remember that our solar system is only a tiny dot within the galaxy to which we belong, the Milky Way. To form an idea of the size of our galaxy, we need to use two different measurements of space. The first is the "light year," which is the distance which light travels in one year, at the velocity of 300,000 kilometers per second. The other is the "parsec," which is the enormous distance of 206,265 astronomical units (a.u.).[14]

The luminous bodies which we can see with our naked eye on a starry night belong to our Milky Way, which has about one hundred billion stars, many of which are up to a million times brighter than our Sun.[15] Light takes about

125,000 light years to cross from one extreme to the other of the Milky Way. The diameter of the Milky Way is some 30,000 parsecs, or 200,000 light years. The approximate distance to the nearest galaxies is about 10,000,000 million light years, and they are moving away from one another at an incredible speed.[16] These distances exceed even our power of imagination, yet Isaiah declares that God measured the vast universe with the palm of His hand. This is how great is our Lord, and even greater, worthy of all praise and worship! Continuing with the thought of the divine greatness, Isaiah adds, *"Lebanon is not sufficient for altar fires, nor its animals enough for burnt offerings."*[17] In his letter to the Colossians, Paul our Lord Jesus Christ as the center and sustainer of all that we see, and of all that we do not see; He sustains all that exists. Our God is marvelous, majestic, and infinitely great. How big is your God? Really, He is the size that you consider Him to be. Let us retain in our thoughts the truth of the greatness of the Lord, and we will be able to act in harmony with that truth. We will conclude this section with the words of the apostle Paul in his letter to Timothy, when full of emotion and gratitude he says:

"Now to the King eternal, immortal, invisible, the only God, be honor and glory for ever and ever. Amen."[18]

Satan and Greatness

Since we have inquired about the greatness of God, let's do the same regarding Satan. He is neither omniscient, omnipotent, nor omnipresent, as we sometimes make him out to be. As far as his power goes, I think that our concept has swung from one extreme of the pendulum to the other. Sometimes we believe him to be a defenseless little creature that we can tread upon, lock in a box and throw away the key. At other times we attribute to him powers and actions that only God has or can do. Since he is in the category of the angels, Satan is greater than human beings; and there is no doubt that he has the power to ruin our lives, if we allow him to do so. On the other hand, we know that the Lord Jesus Christ defeated him through His death and resurrection. Since Jesus is the Head of the Church, she overcomes Satan in the name of her Lord. I believe what Dr. Neil Anderson teaches when he says that Satan's power is based in the mind. Although he is defeated, he makes us think that he is victorious, and at certain times he causes us to fear him more than God, or to ignore him as if he did not exist. To face Satan, more than power we need to declare the truth, since his kingdom of lies melts before the power of the truth.[19] The New Testament presents Satan as "the prince of this world," "the strong man," "the accuser," and "the father of lies," among other descriptions.

What might Satan's sin have been? Without hesitation we can state that it was pride, accompanied by arrogance. The uncontrolled desire to be great, the greatest and most important. The Scriptures in Isaiah 14:12-21 and Ezekiel 28-12-19 describe the fall of a king of Babylon, in the first text, and of a king of Tyre, in the second. These kings, conceited because of the strength and splendor of their kingdoms, attempted to place themselves on the level of God. But these narratives also appear to recount the fall of the guardian cherub. Myer Perlman comments on these prophecies of Isaiah and Ezekiel, "...they drew back the veil of the distant *past and presented the fall of the rebellious angel who said, 'I will make myself like the Most High.' The lesson was as follows: if God punished the blasphemous pride of this exalted angel, He will not fail to punish any monarch who dares to usurp the place of God.''*[20] The passage in Isaiah 14:12-14 reads:

> *How you have fallen from heaven, O morning star, son of the dawn! You have been cast down to the earth, you who once laid low the nations! You said in your heart, "I will ascend to heaven; I will raise my throne above the stars of God; I will sit enthroned on the mount of assembly, on the utmost heights of the sacred mountain. I will ascend above the tops of the clouds; I will make myself like the Most High."*

The description which Ezekiel gives states that this angel had the best of everything. He was perfect, he walked upon the holy mount of God and was in God's very presence, but he wanted more. He desired and aspired to receiving divine worship, but was cast down to the earth. These narratives, as we have seen, constitute a solemn warning for every proud heart, for whether or not they describe the fall of Satan, they show the final end of those who want to be like God, usurping His place. But it is not difficult to understand that these verses refer to Satan, since the characteristic elements of those who want to be great are found in him. In the Garden of Eden he sold the same idea to Eve. The serpent said to her, *"You will be like God, knowing good and evil."*[21] Satan also attempted to get Jesus Himself to worship him, when tempting Him, he showed to Him the kingdoms of the world and said, *"All this I will give you,…if you will bow down and worship me."*[22]

Dr. Billy Graham, referring to the narrative of Isaiah, talks about the five fancies of Lucifer. He lists them: "I will ascend to heaven," "I will raise my throne above the stars of God," "I will sit enthroned on the mount of assembly," "I will ascend above the tops of the clouds," "I will make myself like the Most High." I...I...I...I...I.[23] Satan has created his own kingdom, a dark, evil kingdom of antichrist. He is now, as the Bible calls him, "the prince of demons," and "the ruler of the kingdom of the air." But Lucifer has been defeated, and his destiny is the lake of fire. It should not surprise us that the teaching that we are gods is central to the "New Age Movement." This heresy has been penetrating very subtly in some evangelical Christian congregations. Beware, we are not gods, nor do we deserve God's glory, which He will not share with anyone. We are His creatures, His adopted children through the saving sacrifice of the Lord Jesus Christ. As His disciples, we give glory to Him, the only God, the personal God. Let us imitate the example of our Master, being humble, not proud, for: *"Pride is not greatness, but rather a swelling; and that which is swollen appears great, but it is not healthy."* (Saint Augustine)[24]

Mankind and Greatness

By means of the mind of Christ, we can know who is truly great before God. We become capable of understanding the concept of greatness that the Lord values, and consequently we are able to please the Father in this area also. As we have seen, the longing for greatness and the desire for power can come accompanied by many evils. The history of humanity is full of cases like these, in which the thirst for power has been the sinister, hidden motivation behind the worst moments that the human race has lived through. The most monstrous acts, the most reprehensible deceits and treasons have sprung from this uncontrollable, burning desire to be served by others and to possess power. This feeling can become an evil force that consumes the bones, undermines morality, and destroys the soul. It is an over-whelming force capable of awakening the worst human passions. The Biblical narrative shows that, from Adam to Saul, and from David to the time of Jesus Christ, the passion for greatness has turned noble kings into crowned monsters. Richard J. Foster, speaking of this, says, *"Power has profound consequences in our interpersonal and social relations and our relationship with God. There is nothing that influences us more deeply—whether for good or ill—than power."*[25]

Human examples in this regard are scarcely worth imitating. At the beginning of human history we see Adam and Eve, seduced and deceived by the idea of "being like God," and rejecting the great privilege of being God's creatures. They did not appreciate everything that they were and that they had. They lost their greatest riches, their intimate relationship with God, and all for nothing. The truth is that our dark passions for greatness always end in broken communications and friendship. How sad to see old friends destroying their relationship of many years in a blind struggle for an office or executive position. The French writer Ernest Renan captured this truth in two eloquent sayings: "Kingdoms and fortunes never wish for companions," and "Two dogs with a bone between them are never friends."[26]

This same struggle for power frequently occurs in the home. The man says that he is the head of the house and that therefore he is in charge. And the woman retorts that if the man is the head, she is the neck, and that the head always does what the neck wants. But when God says that the man is the head of the woman, He is not giving to the man a means to satisfy his thirst for power. He is the head; this is his ministry, his responsibility; but he must fulfill it following the example of Christ with His Church, that is, in total giving of himself for his beloved, to the point of sacrifice. The woman is told to submit herself to one man (not to all men), who has bound her with chains of love, a man who loves her as Christ loved His Church. There is no room for despotism here, no place for the tyranny of the man. Commenting on the passage following Ephesians 5:22, Tom Eisenman says:

> (The woman) is not being told here to be obedient to her husband. There is no New Testament verse that describes the relationship of the wife to the husband as one characterized by obedience. But she is being asked to yield her powers to her husband who has already yielded his powers to her. It is love, not control, that is the issue.[27]

As we can see, it is a giving of oneself because of love which demands a submission in love. But what was Jesus' teaching about power and greatness? Do our concepts agree with those of our Lord? Let's look at what He taught His disciples. The apostles, just as human as we are, when they understood whose disciples they were, when they thought of their eternal inheritance, were intrigued

Dr. Daniel Villa

by the question about which of them would be the greatest in the heavenly kingdom. Undoubtedly, this was a very human question. No one was interested in or concerned about who would be the least, since we like to stand out and be first. In the account in Mark 9:33-37 we are told that when the Lord asked the disciples about the topic of their conversation, they were silent. Although Jesus knew their thoughts, He wanted a statement from them. Their silence revealed their understanding that their attitude had not been correct. Jesus surprised them with His concept of greatness and power. He told them, *"If anyone wants to be first, he must be the very last, and the servant of all."*[28] Greatness, according to Jesus, is determined by service. It is this ability to serve which makes us great before God, although it may humiliate us before men. Service destroys pride and vanity. Jesus shows us a fresh, new, special, and revolutionary way to approach greatness. He says to us, "Do you want to be great? Well, humble yourself and serve." *"For he who is least among you all—he is the greatest."*[29] What a paradox He presents us here! This can only be understood through the mind of Christ within us. If we do not understand it or practice it, we will be struggling to stand out and to feel that we have power, even though we have to step on the heads of our brothers and sisters to achieve it. Be careful, let us remember that *"Power is like the walnut tree; it allows nothing to grow within its shadow"* (Antonio Gala, a Spanish writer).[30]

The Guests at the Wedding Feast

Luke is the only Gospel that records the incident when the people invited to a wedding feast were contending for the most important places. When Jesus saw this, He used the occasion to teach His disciples.

When someone invites you to a wedding feast, do not take the place of honor, for a person more distinguished than you may have been invited. If so, the host who invited both of you will come and say to you, "Give this man your seat." Then, humiliated, you will have to take the least important place. But when you are invited, take the lowest place, so that when your host comes, he will say to you, "Friend, move up to a better place." Then you will be honored in the presence of all your fellow guests. For everyone who exalts himself will be humbled, and he who humbles himself will be exalted.[31]

We should point out that the Teacher was not simply giving a lesson in courtesy or prudence; He was sharing a fundamental principle of the Kingdom of Heaven, that is, humility. The central places at the table were considered more important; therefore honor was attributed to those seated there. There were also intermediate places, and others of least importance; so if the host found an important guest in a position of lower honor, he would ask him to move to a more important position. Everett Harrison quotes Plummer, who points out that a general principle is stated here: *"Humility is the dossier for obtaining promotions in the Kingdom of God.*[32] This truth runs contrary to normal procedures in our society, where cleverness, treachery, and playing dirty are used to rise to positions of power. But in the Kingdom of God things are not like that; so the citizens of the Kingdom of heaven should not practice these evils. Jesus expounds in a gracious, masterly way the teaching of Proverbs 25:6-7, which says, *"Do not exalt yourself in the king's presence, and do not claim a place among great men; it is better for him to say to you, 'Come up here,' than for him to humiliate you before a nobleman.*" Bengel, quoted by Jamieson, makes an interesting point: "To take the lowest place is ignominious only to him who aspires to the highest." Here it appears that we confront the heavenly concept of greatness and honor, and how to attain them. Jesus teaches us, *"Everyone who exalts himself will be humbled, and he who humbles himself will be exalted."*[33] Let us humble ourselves and become aware of the danger represented by pride and arrogance. Let us avoid seeking public recognition and promotion of ourselves and our ministries. Let us allow God to make known to men what we are in secret. The Latin historian Cursio Rufo Quinto once said, *"The deepest rivers are always the quietest."*[34]

The Petition of James and John

Here we have a most interesting situation, since it reveals to us two different angles of the spiritual growth of the disciples. We find the account in Matthew 20:20-28, Mark 10:35-45, and Luke 22:24-30. The Bible tells us that James and John, backed by their mother, petitioned the Lord Jesus that the privilege of sitting one on His right and the other on His left should be assigned to them in the heavenly kingdom. We might ask how this mother and two of the three most intimate disciples could dare to make such a request, to occupy the most important places in the Kingdom, since Jesus' teachings and His daily example had warned them against such attitudes. [35]But we would be forced to admit that after almost two thousand years of the preaching of the gospel, we still have not learned to think as Jesus thinks about greatness and humility. Those teachings about not holding too high an opinion of oneself, or the denial of self and the principle of service, sadly, even today, are not fully realized in us, and in their place the old nature appears to reign. Let's review the Biblical account and find out first hand what happened:

> Then the mother of Zebedee's sons came to Jesus with her sons and, kneeling down, asked a favor of him. "What is it you want?" he asked. She said, "Grant that one of these two sons of mine may sit at your right and the other at your left in your kingdom." "You don't know what you are asking," Jesus said to them. "Can you drink the cup I am going to drink?" "We can," they answered. Jesus said to them, "You will indeed drink from my cup, but to sit at my right or left is not for me to grant. These places belong to those for whom they have been prepared by my Father." When the ten heard about this, they were indignant with the two brothers. Jesus called them together and said, "You know that the rulers of the Gentiles lord it over them, and their high officials exercise authority over them. No so with you. Instead, whoever wants to become great among you must be your servant, and whoever wants to be first must be your slave—just as the Son of Man did not come to be served, but to serve, and to give his life as a ransom for many.[36]

The Boanerges men likely asked their mother to make her request, but what is absolutely certain is that they were totally in agreement with it. These two brothers later on proved that they were ready to drink from the Lord's cup. James was the first of the apostles to die, and his brother John suffered severe persecution against the church and exile. He was the last of the apostles to die. In spite of this request, they were sincere believers, and it is likely that they repented many times having made the petition. We note that Jesus did not say that those positions would not be given to them, rather that they were for those chosen by the Father. Could they perhaps be those chosen ones? Why not? The other disciples became angry with the two brothers. They obviously knew that the attitude of the Boanerges was not correct. What the brothers were really asking for was greater honor, the most important seats after Jesus Himself. And, as G. Hendriksen says, *"They forget that a prayer that asks for glory is a prayer that asks for suffering.*[37] That is why Jesus asked them whether they were willing to drink from His cup.

The Lord said to His disciples, *"It will not be so among you,"* referring to the way that unbelievers act. Jesus Christ gave us His example so that we might imitate Him, and instead of desiring to be great and renowned on earth we should strive to attain these things in the Kingdom. Jesus said, *"just as the Son of Man did not come to be served, but to serve, and to give his life as a ransom for many."* We do well to remember that Jesus Christ did not acquire His name and Kingdom by His mighty deeds. He already had those things. Our heroes arise from the masses and attain a great name and demand to be served. Our King has always been a king. Jesus laid aside His glory and majesty in order to save us and teach us to live like Him. Jesus' words must have seemed difficult and hard to accept to His disciples when He said that the Son of Man did not come to be served but to serve. Perhaps one of them said, "Just a minute, Master, you don't know what you are saying. The Son of Man is the leader guide, the triumphant general, He is the hope of liberation." Or, "The Son of Man is greatness personified. How can you say that you did not come to be served?" Or, "It is impossible that you should suffer and die." Or, "You are the hope of Israel and worthy to receive service from all of us." If any of the disciples said anything like this, he was completely correct. And herein lies the greatness of our Lord. He who deserved to be served came to serve. What about you?

Our experience with our public authorities confirms Jesus' observation. Our politicians aspire to public office with the apparent aim of serving their people, but once in power in most cases the roles are inverted. They forget the people, and instead of serving, they ask to be served. But Jesus Christ says to His disciples, *"It will not be so among you."* Once more the doctrines and norms of the Kingdom shine forth and are presented tenderly but firmly by the King of kings. Once again our concepts of greatness are shaken by the principles of the Kingdom of Heaven. *"If anyone wants to be first, he must be the very last, and the servant of all."* This is only fully understood by means of the mind of Christ in us. And when we understand it, we ought then to aspire to be great in the Kingdom of Heaven. The Church needs such men and women. [38]

Chapter 6
GOD AND TIME

"He has made everything beautiful in its time."
Ecclesiastes 3:11

She arrived at our church one Sunday morning because of an invitation that a member of the church had left at her door during a visitation effort that we had made in our neighborhood. She was an intelligent young woman, restless, inquisitive and with spiritual hunger. To protect her identity I will call her Jessica; she was single and held an important position with a well-known business in the city. Jessica had previously made a decision for Christ; her spiritual growth was rapid, and she began to accept responsibilities that the church offered to her. Our church had a continuous, strong missionary emphasis, and so this young woman came to identify herself with and love missions. She joined missionary prayer groups and attended the missionary conventions, participating in all such events that she could.

On one occasion our city was visited by the ship "Logos" of Operation Mobilization, a missionary organization which trains young people on its ships, while they sail to many ports and preach the gospel. We talked to Jessica about helping this effort by serving as part of their support team on shore, and she did so. The organization customarily recruits personnel in each port it visits. Jessica wanted to join the team on board the Logos.

She came to me very excited and said, "Pastor, God is calling me to missions, and I have decided to leave shortly with the Logos." The circumstances of our sister's life were such that we did not think that it was an appropriate time for her to leave. But she was confused. If the Lord was calling her, how could she not respond? None of us doubted God's call to Jessica. The question was, when? Yes, when did the Lord want her to leave for the mission field? Our natural response is, Immediately, because the need is great. Undoubtedly, the Lord calls us because the world needs to hear the saving message of Jesus, but He takes time to prepare us and then He sends us. Even after the disciples had spent much time with Him, and in spite of the need, He told them to wait in Jerusalem until they received the power from on high.

How would you define time? Believe me, it is not easy to do, since we use time to measure time. The concept of time may appear abstract, but the results of its passing are all too concrete. The Bible tells us that everything upon earth has its moment and its opportunity to be realized. Its exact words are, *"There is a time for everything, and a season for every activity under heaven."*[1] How certain, profound, and wise are these words! For every desire or purpose there exists an appropriate moment in which we can attain it. It is like saying, "Grapes will ripen at their proper time," not before or later, but in their proper season. Undoubtedly, this is part of what God teaches us about time. So we should ask ourselves, Is our concept of time similar to that of God? The apostle Peter tells us that we should not forget that *with the Lord a day is like a thousand years, and a thousand years are like a day.*[2] Here he refers to the eternity of God, who is not subject to time and space as are we. And what appears to us to be a long wait is only a moment for God. Through the mind of Christ in us we can understand this truth, and so remain blessed in our waiting and unshaken in our hope. I once read an item titled "Heavenly humor." It goes like this: A man was trying to understand the nature of God and was asking Him questions. "Lord, what are a million years to you?" God answered, "A million years are like one minute." Then the man asked, "Lord, how much are a million dollars to you?" to which God replied, "A million dollars are like one cent." The man thought a moment and then asked, "Lord, will you give me one cent?" And God answered, "Just a minute."[3]

We should remember that our purpose is not to try to guess what God will do. Rather we should trust ourselves into His hands, in full assurance of faith that He is in control, that our God never finds Himself in a crisis, and that He is dependably punctual. He arrives at the exact moment, not before or after. This is God's concept of time.

Israel's wait for the promised Messiah appeared to indicate forgetfulness of the part of God. The practice followed by some of expecting in each childbirth the appearance of the longed-for Redeemer was a testimony to their hope in the midst of general hopelessness. But the apostle Paul, without hesitation boldly states, *"When the time had fully come, God sent his Son, born of a woman, born under law.'*[4] It happened when the time was fulfilled, not before and not afterward. To the Israelites it appeared to be delayed, but not to God. With Him there are no delays nor lateness, for to our Lord every hour is an eternal present. I should complete my story and tell you that Jessica continued to grow and mature. Some years later she met a young man that loved missions as much as she did; they were married and went as missionaries to Spain. Today they are preparing to become career missionaries. For us, who live under the control of time, it will help us greatly to understand God's concept of time. To forget it might change completely the divine plan for our lives. Let us look at the story of sincere men of God, to see how their history was shaped by their understanding or ignorance of this truth.

Abraham: His Call and His Descendents
(Hope in the midst of hopelessness)

As with all believers, the Lord blessed Abraham so that he would become a blessing to others. God chose the patriarch through pure, abundant grace. The Messianic line beginning with Adam led first to Shem and continued to Abraham. When God called him, He promised to make him the father of a great nation. The problem was that this mature man had no children.

The divine promise given to the patriarch, which included his wife Sarah, pointed out the great misfortune of this rich couple, the lack of children. In order for the promise to be fulfilled, it was necessary to remove Sarah's "reproach," her barrenness. But might this infertility have been part of God's plan for Abraham in allowing him to marry his half-sister? Could this have been planned by God in His omniscience as a way to reveal His power? In oriental societies barrenness was considered a divine curse. No doubt this was a serious concern for Abraham and Sarah.

We can find three attempts to resolve the lack of an heir. We think the first was the decision to take Lot, the orphan nephew, with them to the land which God would show them. But God's command had been to leave their birthplace and family. It is probable that they intended to adopt Lot as their son, a very common practice in those days. But this plan appears to have failed because of the attitude of Lot and his eventual separation from Abraham and Sarah.

1 Tay

We find the second attempt in the oriental custom of adopting a servant born in the household. Abraham expressed this to the Lord, when he lamented about the need to do so. *"Abram said, 'You have given me no children; so a servant in my household will be my heir.' Then the word of the Lord came to him: 'This man will not be your heir, but a son coming from your own body will be your heir.'"*[5] As we see, this possibility ends because of the word from God. Here the Lord specifies that this great number of descendents will come through his own son (not one adopted). The word from the Lord revived Abraham's lost hope of having a son.

Let's look at the third attempt. When God called Abraham, he was already seventy-five years old.[6] Don't you

Dr. Daniel Villa

agree that if God is going to give a son to a man of seventy-five, He ought to do so in the shortest possible time? Perhaps so, but God's time is different from ours. The divine, eternal concept of time seeks to mature us and prepare us until the exact instant when we are truly ready to live that moment. Ten years after the departure from Haran, chapter 16 tells us that Sarah was still barren. For this reason she became desperate and like many of us, she began to suggest ideas to the Most High, giving Him the help that she thought He needed. Just as we despair as we see time pass, and what we long for, and in some cases what God has promised us, does not arrive. We think that we have waited long enough, and that if God is going to act, He should do so immediately. And we say, " If He is really going to do this, this is the time. I don't have any more strength. I can't wait any longer." And seeing that although we have waited, nothing is happening, we begin to solve the problem ourselves in an attempt to help the Lord. Isn't it true that we act this way, exactly as Sarah did? Perhaps she presented her idea like this: "Well, Abraham, God told you that you will have a family through your own son, but He didn't say anything about me. It must be that it will be a son that you father and that legally will be our son," and then with a shout of joy, "Of course! Now I see. I've got it! I've got it!" "What are you talking about?" Abraham might have answered, somewhat confused. With sparkling eyes and a joyful expression she said, "Remember Hagar, my slave? She can give you a son. If you take her, she will conceive and her son will be mine. That's the law!" "This must be the way in which the Lord will give us an heir." "Let's do it," they probably both said, very excited. Perhaps it didn't happen exactly this way, but something similar obviously took place. We know the rest of the story. Abraham took the slave Hagar and she conceived.[7]And from that very moment this hasty action began to produce problems. Hagar began to look down on Sarah, which caused Sarah to be jealous of her slave. The situation got worse when Hagar bore her son Ishmael, and the baby stole the heart of his elderly father. The conflict in the home became so severe that finally Abraham had to send away Hagar and her son from the family.

Abraham and Sarah became desperate and tried to help God. But what they did was not in the timing nor the plan of God. The same thing happens to us today when in our impatience we seek options which appear acceptable to us but which are not part of God's plan. They won't work, believe me that they won't work! Something will happen, but the result will not be the exact, excellent will of God. From the aforementioned union was born Ishmael, the father of the Ishmaelites, the powerful Arab world. Throughout history the rivalry between the Arabs and the Jews has cost hundreds of thousands of human lives in many wars. And in a historic mixture of political, religious, economic and military aspects, the so-called "Christian world" faced off against the "Muslim world" in a series of bloody wars known as "The Crusades." It was the cross against the crescent. Sad to say, the hatred and shedding of blood between Jews and Arabs continues in the present. It is truly an international conflict which keeps the Middle East like a time bomb, begun by the impatience of one couple. But not only strictly human aspects such as the religious and political dimensions are involved, but also a spiritual conflict is playing out, as real and serious as those others. The religion of the Arabs is Islam, which today constitutes the great bastion of the enemies of the gospel of Jesus Christ. Many places where the gospel was sown and which became strongholds of Christianity, are today fortresses of Islam, where to preach about Jesus is a crime. The seven churches mentioned in the beginning of the Book of Revelation are an example of this. (Those churches were located in Asia Minor, which was conquered in 1071 by the Seljuk Turks, who were converts to Islam. Asia Minor is today Turkey.[8]) When we observe this story, we realize how important it is to move in God's timing.

When Ishmael was born Abraham was 86 years old and Sarah was about ten years younger. Genesis chapter 16 tells us that it was not until thirteen years after the birth of Ishmael that the Lord spoke to Abraham again about his heir. On this occasion He promised him specifically a son from his marriage, a son by Sarah. And we ask, Why so long afterwards? Was the divine plan delayed by the precipitous action of this couple? Can we, in our hurry to see God work, stop or delay His action? What is certain is that there were some thirteen years of divine silence on the subject. The Lord waited until all the alternatives available to Abraham and Sarah had evaporated. Their last hope had been Ishmael, but they were told that the promise of descendents would come through a son of both of them. The birth of Isaac did not happen until all human possibilities had been exhausted. When it was simply impossible, the Lord told the patriarch that Sarah would conceive; and this overthrew the third attempt to solve the problem. This happened exactly twenty-five years after the first promise was given. Incredible! That's our God!

Abraham did not believe what he was hearing, and he even requested that the blessing be given to Ishmael. The Lord had to insist upon His plan. Let's look at the biblical account.

> God also said to Abraham, "As for Sarai your wife, you are no longer to call her Sarai; her name will be Sarah. I will bless her so that she will be the mother of nations; kings of peoples will come from her." Abraham fell face-down; he laughed and said to himself, "Will a son be born to a man a hundred years old? Will Sarah bear a child at the age of ninety?" And Abraham said to God, "If only Ishmael might live under your blessing!" Then God said, "Yes, but your wife Sarah will bear you a son, and you will call him Isaac. I will establish my covenant with him as an everlasting covenant for his descendants after him. And as for Ishmael, I have heard you; I will surely bless him; I will make him fruitful and will greatly increase his numbers…. But my covenant I will establish with Isaac, whom Sarah will bear to you by this time next year."[9]

Together with this promise, the Lord changed the names of both Abraham and Sarah, because they would be the parents of multitudes. Sarah also did not believe God, and like her husband and half-brother, she laughed at the divine promise, since she thought that at her age it was impossible for her to conceive. It is as if she were saying, "God, you came too late; this time you are too late." But

PATIENCE!

Dr. Daniel Villa

for our Lord nothing is impossible. Just as it was said to her, Sarah conceived and bore Isaac, whose name means laughter. After waiting twenty-five years and overcoming all opposition, God did this. He does not need our help; He asks only our trust. He does not ask for our cooperation, only our patience. Will you do this? As you wait for what God has promised you, do you still have human alternatives? In other words, are you suggesting ideas to God? In my own experience I find that whenever I mark a door as my exit, the Lord always opens another.

By means of the mind of Christ within us we can understand the divine concept of time, and we are able to maintain our trust in the midst of despair. Faith makes us children that trust their powerful, loving Father, for we proceed holding His hand. We become capable of hope, even when it appears that we must despair. Our heavenly Father will never give us a stone when we ask for bread, nor a serpent when we are asking for fish. We will trust our Lord. And like children we can remember that song for children that says:

> When I pray, God sometimes answers Yes.
> When I pray, God sometimes answers Wait,
> And sometimes No, because He loves me.
> But God always answers my prayer.

Moses: His Scepter and His Rod

Moses is one of the greatest, if not the greatest personage of the Old Testament. The Sacred Text presents him as leader, prince, shepherd, patriarch, liberator, judge, legislator, governor, conqueror, military strategist, national hero, prophet, priest, composer of psalms, biblical author, and the meekest man on earth.

The life of Moses included such dissimilar paths as the royal palace and the burning desert. His history can be divided into three periods of forty years each. In the first he was a prince of Egypt in the house of Pharaoh. In the second he tended a flock of sheep for forty years in the desert of Midian. In the third he spent forty years in active ministry as liberator and leader of the people of Israel.

In this history the concept of time is extremely fascinating and revealing, for God spent eighty years preparing Moses, in order to use him for forty years. When we read of all that this man accomplished for his Lord, his mighty deeds, his steps of faith, and his unfailing submission to the will of God, we understand that he was a man made ready in an unhurried preparation, forged in the slow fire of the divine patience.

Deuteronomy 34:7 and 10-12 says this about Moses:

Moses was a hundred and twenty years old when he died, yet his eyes were not weak nor his strength gone.... Since then, no prophet has risen in Israel like Moses, whom the Lord knew face to face, who did all those miraculous signs and wonders the Lord sent him to do in Egypt—to Pharaoh and to all his officials and to his whole land. For no one has ever shown the mighty power or performed the awesome deeds that Moses did in the sight of all Israel.

Let us look in detail at these three periods in the life of this man, and the divine lesson that he learned in each.

Forty Years in Pharaoh's House

When Joseph was the second ruler of Egypt under the Pharaoh, the Hebrews were received peacefully in Egypt as a large family; they numbered a few more than seventy-six people.[10] As God had foretold to Jacob, the Hebrews multiplied greatly in Egypt, becoming more numerous than the Egyptians themselves. The Bible's words are, *"The land was filled with them."*[11] The king of Egypt in those days was one "who had not known Joseph;" he became alarmed and decided to take measures to protect the security of his nation, and so began to mistreat and subjugate the Hebrews to the point of making slaves of them. But they still continued to multiply dangerously. Then the decree went out that all the Hebrew boy babies that were born should be killed, allowing only the girl babies to live.

The Book of Hebrews chapter 11 tells us that it was by faith that Moses' parents refused to obey the royal decree and decided to try to preserve the life of their newborn boy, placing him in a basket and trusting him to the river. Their faith was rewarded, for the child was providentially taken from the river and adopted by the sister of the king; and Moses' own mother was called to feed and care for him. This period was one of double learning for Moses, because he was instructed not only in the life of the palace but also in the faith of his forefathers. His mother shared with him the truths about his God, his race, and the divine promises which they held, so that the young Moses grew up knowing the true God. On the other hand, he also received royal education and training. This gave him access to the best knowledge of the time: the sciences, arts, and warfare. Military training and the techniques and strategies of war were doubtless part of the preparation of a prince, in that period when warfare was a way of life.

Those first forty years produced a man who was strong, robust, and healthy. He had been educated with the greatest care, as befitting a prince, competent in the arts of warfare and governance. But he was also a man who knew his roots and his culture, a believer in the God of Abraham, Isaac, and Jacob, a man who was prepared to hear the voice of God. Moses identified himself more with the oppressed than with the oppressors. We ought not to think that Moses grew up not knowing who he was nor to what race he belonged. On the contrary, it is very likely that his parents had imparted to him the idea that perhaps he might be the one that God would raise up to liberate his people. There is no doubt that at the age of forty Moses knew that he was the one chosen for the liberation of his people; and it appears that then he attempted to do so through his own efforts, and killed the Egyptian who was beating an Israelite. Perhaps he felt himself to be a Messiah or champion or superhero. About this incident the Bible says, *"Moses thought that his own people would realize that God was using him to rescue them, but they did not."*[12] Moses was rejected by his own people, and then began to realize how "impossible" this task was, as well as the difficult, contradictory nature of that people. Disillusioned, sad, and defeated, he fled to the desert.

What thoughts must have traveled with him on that long, hard road? Had God really called him to this task? If that were so, why did he have to lose his distinguished, privileged position in Egyptian society? Would it not be easier to reach his goal by means of the influence he had had in Egypt and with the king? How was it that his own people could not understand his mission? How could they not see the great sacrifice which he was making for them? Whether he had these thoughts, and even harsher ones, we do not know, but any mortal would have thought them.

Forty Years in the Desert of Midian

Now as a fugitive from justice, Moses flees from Egypt and takes refuge among the Midianites, who were descendents of Abraham and who worshiped the true God. Jethro was the priest and governor of that region.[13] Moses helps the daughters of Jethro when they faced hostile shepherds. Once again he acts to rescue the weak and oppressed. That is how he enters Jethro's household and consents to live with the family. He married one of the daughters and had two children with her. How difficult those first years in the strange land must have been! Perhaps at the door of his tent or while tending the flock, his mind would travel back to his days in the court of the Pharaoh. He no longer wore his royal robes and ornaments, but the memories were fresh in his mind. How difficult it must have been for him to adapt to his new and oh so different lifestyle. He would miss the social whirl of Egypt, with its delicious foods, the great halls and corridors and apartments of the palace. He had given up all this because of his divine vocation, and perhaps he wondered, why? With the passage of time perhaps Moses began to forget that former life, and the peoples with whom he had associated, and his calling.

Although the Lord had called Moses, laying on his heart the heavy burden for his people so miserably enslaved, and in spite of the superior Egyptian education which he had received, Moses was not ready to fulfill the divine plan. Our patient Lord waited all the time necessary for Moses to become ready. But were not the people of Israel suffering? Did God not see their affliction? Undoubtedly He did, but He did not send their liberator until the fullness of time. He used the exile in Midian to shape the man to His exact standards.

What did Moses learn? I believe that during his journey on the path of exile, God broke him completely. God took from him his royal robes, his servants, and his scepter (symbol of his authority as a prince). He blasted his face with the sand of the desert. He allowed him to feel the burning sun on his body and the tormenting thirst in his throat. The only thing that fugitive could do was trust in his God. His pride and self-sufficiency lay buried beneath the burning desert sands. The Lord taught Moses to depend on Him. He also learned the patience, and the meticulous care needed to shepherd sheep. In the quiet of the mountains and plains the Lord taught him what he could not have learned in the palace. God was preparing him to struggle with a people that the Lord Himself called "stubborn." Moses came to know very well all the region bordering the Gulf of Aqaba, through which years later he would lead the Israelites. God took the prince and made him a shepherd. In place of a place, He gave him the mountains of a barren desert. He exchanged his royal robes for a rod, a shepherd's staff, and He changed the violent Hebrew into "the meekest man on earth." Now Moses was ready for his difficult task, and he received a direct call to his mission, after exactly forty years

Forty Years in Active Ministry

Exodus chapter 3 tells us of the direct or formal call which the Lord gave to Moses. God appeared to him in the midst of a bush that was enveloped in flames but which was not consumed. When God revealed Himself and told Moses His intention to send him to Egypt to liberate Israel, we would have expected a positive, enthusiastic response, in the light of Moses' former patriotic fervor. However, when the Lord confronts him with the call, we see a man who believes himself incapable of this task, and who trembles at the mere thought of it. This attitude shows to us that he really was ready. In general it is a good sign when, facing the divine call, we are overcome by feelings of fear and inadequacy, because they force us into total dependence upon God, which is His intention. Moses presented his best excuses to the Lord, and one by one they were refuted. Exodus chapters 3 and 4 tell the story. Moses said to the Lord, "Who am I to present myself before Pharaoh and bring the Israelites out of Egypt?" God answered that He would be with Moses, who would lead the people out to worship the Lord in that very mountain. Here we observe a different Moses, a man who knows himself to be without resources. This is the man that God will use in powerful ways to liberate His people from their slavery.

The ministry of Moses was replete with signs and wonders from the hand of God on behalf of His people, ordered by the direct command of Moses. We recall the plagues in Egypt, the crossing of the Red Sea, the rock that provided water for the people, and the column of fire which guided them by night and the cloud by day. It was to Moses that the Lord delivered the tables of the Law, written by the finger of God.

Moses was, without question, the one who forged the nation of Israel. This people had never lived as a formally organized nation, for they had never had the occasion to do so. The relationships within this people were more in the nature of a family than of a nation; in fact, in the first verses of the Book of Exodus, they are spoken of only as "the children of Israel." When they were segregated and enslaved, their class identity or nationality became more clear. They were different, they were Israelites. They were distinguished by their race, their history, their faith, their sufferings. But the transformation which occurred during that journey of the Hebrew people was extraordinary. Moses leads out of slavery in Egypt a group with very rudimentary organization, but God shapes it into a true people. In Sinai the Lord gives them a constitution which will govern them as a nation. He gave them commandments and ordinances which would shape the life of every citizen. They received a code of ethics and both moral and civil laws. He instituted a judicial system for them. He gave them laws for slave owners, laws about acts of violence, laws regulating the responsibility of masters and owners, laws about restitution: humanitarian laws. He taught them their religion and how to practice it, how to be faithful to God by means of His fundamental principles. He also established their religious festivals, and their place of worship and gathering. He chose priests for them and established ceremonies to practice and to become tradition generation after generation. Unquestionably, he gave them a sense of belonging, he made them a people; he organized their army and gave them their King.

Great and glorious was the labor performed by Moses for the glory of God and the benefit of his people. Why did he not do it previously? He did it precisely at the proper time. The mind of Christ in us permits us to understand this. To my mind come the stories of brothers and sisters called by the Lord to diverse ministries. Some of these people were used immediately by the Lord, but others did not begin their task for three, four, or even five years after receiving their call. Perhaps it depends on the person and the ministry to which he was called by God. This is the divine concept of time, and there is a blessing in understanding it.

David: Waiting to Become King

David, the second human king of Israel, was an extraordinary man: of renowned valor, ingenious, a born leader, fair, god-fearing, a shepherd, harp player, singer, psalmist, prophet, and a man after God's own heart. To him God promised an eternal kingdom through his descendants which culminate in Jesus Christ, King of kings and Lord of lords. The humble shepherd, the son of Jesse, was undoubtedly a most outstanding man of his generation, and the most important king of Israel. His life was so formative in Hebrew history, and considering the Messianic promises, that in the time of Jesus the title "Son of David" became a synonym for "Messiah." The author and ex-president of the Dominican Republic, Juan Bosch, in his book *David, Biografía de un Rey*, sums up in these words his eventful and unusual life: *"...David ben Isaí (his Hebrew name), who moved from being a shepherd to military captain and son-in-law of King Saul, from there to being a fugitive, leader of an armed company, a vassal ally of the Philistines, king of Judah and of Israel, conqueror of Jerusalem and subjugator of nations, and finally, a man of such historic importance that a thousand years after his death, his name would be used by Jesus Christ, who would call Himself the Son of David."*[14]

> To be exact, Jesus did not use this title Himself; He always called Himself "the Son of man"; but He was pleased to accept the title of Son of David when others called Him so.

The "sweet singer of Israel" was another who had to learn the concept of the timing of God. Looking retrospectively, Psalm 78 recounts the divine care for Israel throughout her history and says, *"He chose David his servant and took him from the sheep pens; from tending the sheep he brought him to be the shepherd of his people Jacob, of Israel his inheritance. And David shepherded them with integrity of heart; with skilful hands he led them."* But how much time intervened between his anointing as king and his occupying that position? Would you not suppose that since this was the will of God, that David's path to his proclamation as king would have been bright, smooth, and popularly accepted? But it did not happen that way. The harpist for King Saul, faithful to his calling, did not consider it his responsibility to bring about the fulfillment of the divine promises. Rather he waited for God's time, although that waiting brought him into intense suffering at the hands of Saul ben Cis. The Bible account of the first two kings of Israel is complex. Some of the stories appear to repeat themselves, and it is difficult to establish dates. Nevertheless, let us look briefly at the history of David.

From Shepherd of the Flock to Son-in-law of the King

David was the grandson of Boaz and Ruth the Moabitess, the last of the eight sons of Jesse. He lived in the region of Bethlehem, the territory of the tribe of Judah. From a very early age he lived in the fields, caring for his father's sheep. David was about eighteen to twenty years old when he was called by Saul to sooth him with his music. If that is so, he must have been anointed by Samuel between age twelve and eighteen. This fact is deduced from the fear Samuel manifested when the Lord sent him to Bethlehem to anoint the future king. Samuel said that if Saul found out about his purpose, he would kill him. This fear can be understood after the prophet had broken his relationship with the king, because Saul had been completely rejected by the Lord. This must have happened in the second decade of Saul's forty-year reign.[15]

We must remember that after his anointing, the Scripture tells us, *"From that day on the Spirit of the Lord came upon David in power."* [16]It is very likely that David's brothers did not understand the significance of that anointing, and consequently neither its magnitude nor extent. Once in Saul's household, since the king had no true palace or court, David began to excel, and soon became not only the king's musician but his page at arms. His race to the top was astounding; this harpist to the king showed himself to be a valiant man with a firm trust in the God of Israel. The Lord had lifted him from being a shepherd to a national hero, one of the captains of the king's guard. David no doubt was aware of the divine purpose in shaping him to become the future king of Israel. Up to this point everything was progressing as smoothly as could be desired, but the difficulties soon began. Whether or not motivated by comments and attitudes of David, the king begins to feel jealousy and to see in his young captain a serious threat to his kingdom, a situation made worse by the sincere, intimate friendship between David and Jonathan, the heir to the throne. In a strange move, Saul offered his older daughter in marriage to David, who refused the offer because he did not consider himself worthy. However, some time later David fell in love with Michal, whom he married, thus becoming the king's son-in-law. At the same time that the Spirit of God was with David and he was ascending as a bright light of hope, Saul was abandoned by the Lord, and the king's jealousy toward the son of Jesse was increasing.

From the King's Son-in-law to Royal Fugitive

David was young, handsome, brave, intelligent, with a sharp intuition which enabled him to make quick and accurate decisions. Moreover, he was beloved by the people, respected by the king's servants, son-in-law to the king, and close friend to the crown prince. But the most significant factor for Saul was that he knew that God was with David and was prospering everything he did; for this reason he feared David. The sum of David's exceptional qualities added up to royal jealousy. According to the Biblical narrative, everything began, or came out into the open, when, upon David's return from the battle in which he had killed Goliath, the women of the people received the warriors with singing and dancing. The Bible tells it this way: *"As they danced, they sang: 'Saul has slain his thousands, and David his tens of thousands.' Saul was very angry; this refrain galled him. 'They have credited David with tens of thousands,' he thought, 'but me with only thousands. What more can he get but the kingdom?' And from that time on Saul kept a jealous eye on David."*[17] The joyful naiveté of the women became the detonator for the jealousy of the sixty-something-year-old king.

It is strange that even the positions of power and privilege which David obtained were gained through jealousy and fear which he provoked in the king. For example, when Saul placed him in command of a battalion, he did so to distance David from himself and to keep him busy in warfare, as well, doubtless, to expose him to the risks of combat. It was also for this reason that Saul came up with the idea of making David his son-in-law. *"Saul said to David, 'Here is my older daughter Merab. I will give her to you in marriage; only serve me bravely and fight the battles of the Lord.' For Saul said to himself, 'I will not raise a hand against him. Let the Philistines do that!'"* [18] As we see from the Biblical narrative, Saul had no intention of allowing David to become his son-in-law; David was in fact already a valiant warrior, Saul simply attempted to hide his hatred and cause David's death. When the time came to give his daughter to David in marriage, she was given to someone else. When the king learned that his other daughter Michal was interested in David, he tried to take advantage of this situation as well. He offered her to David as wife, asking as dowry that David kill one hundred Philistines and take him their foreskins. The Scriptures tell us what was in his heart, saying, *"Saul's plan was to have David fall by the hands of the Philistines."* [19]But the grandson of Ruth the Moabitess not only fulfilled the royal request, he doubled it by circumcising two hundred of his dead enemies. The king had no option but to give his daughter to his hated captain. As Bosch comments, this was the moment when Saul should have put an end to his animosity toward David and recognized the valor of his promising young son-in-law. Rather:

> …behold that a man abandoned to his passions is the more the slave to them the greater the power which he exercises over others, for it is not enough for him to command, and it is not enough for him to feel. Saul

> was a slave to his jealousy; he had released a monster within himself, and he could not restrain it.[20]

The Bible tells us that on two occasions Saul attempted to strike David through with his lance while the latter was playing the harp. He made another attempt on David's life when he sent men to kill him while in bed with Princess Michal, who warned him of the danger and saved her husband's life. David understood the deadly threat against him and fled from the king. This was the beginning of a long, shameful manhunt that the crazy, brutish king undertook against the man who would be his successor and the most illustrious king in the entire history of Israel. Saul's pride, combined with his power, proved to be a fatal combination for this first (human) king of Israel. All this should serve as an example to us not to tyrannize those subordinate to us. The leader must never lose perspective as to who he is in truth, and why he is where he is. He is simply a servant. Richard Foster says, *"Pride makes us believe that we are right, and power gives us the ability to force other people to accept our vision of what is right. The marriage of pride and power places us on the very edge of the demonic."*[21]

From Fugitive to King over all Israel

The importance that the son of Jesse should understand and wait patiently for God's timing, as well as the Lord's providential care for him, are very clearly seen in this segment of his life. They were three or four years of wretched living, in which he even had to pretend to be out of his mind to stay alive. He was fleeing from one place to another, with no permanent place to live. He hid in caves and deserts and mountains, in the dread of one who feared being caught and who could not settle anywhere. When he attempted to do so, he had to move on, because he had been found by his enemies. Most of this time he was not fleeing alone, but in the company of his "band" of six hundred men plus their families. David's faith was testing in innumerable ways. His strength was forged and tanned in the sun. God was preparing a king with no hurry whatsoever; He took as much time as He considered necessary.

David fled from Saul and for a time found refuge with Samuel in Ramah. There the Lord protected him, causing the soldiers sent to arrest him, and even the king himself, to fall into a prophetic trance. In his flight David stopped to see the priest Ahimelech, and lied to him, concealing the reason for his visit and receiving help for his escape. This would be the cause of the death of Ahimelech and 85 of his priests and their families. Only Abiathar, the son of Ahimelech, escaped and went to join David.

David had gone to take refuge in the cave of Adullam, and his relatives and friends went to him there, but not only they. *"All those who were in distress or in debt or discontented gathered around him, and he became their leader. About four hundred men were with him."*[22] Thus our subject became the leader of a band that would fight for its survival, and doubtless this was part of God's providential care for David. That army came to number about six hundred men. The jealous acts of King Saul were the instruments which shaped and exalted the figure of the grandson of the Moabitess. As Saul pursued and persecuted David, and even killed because of his jealousy, he progressively disqualified himself to be king, and with his murderous lance, he both aimed at and pointed out the future king of Israel.

It is not unthinkable that by this time Saul knew that the Lord had chosen David as his successor, instead of Jonathan his son, and that Jonathan had accepted this. It was this very fact that caused him to intensify his persecution. The Bible relates the encounter between David and Jonathan and the unusual declaration of the crown prince. Jonathan understood the divine plan and went out to encourage his beleaguered friend. He said to David, *"Don't be afraid…. My father Saul will not lay a hand on you. You will be king over Israel, and I will be second to you. Even my father Saul know this."*[23]

Just as Jonathan had said, God was protecting David from falling into the hands of his pursuer, and always found a way to deliver him from the enemy. I Samuel 23:26-28 tells us that Saul and his troops had surrounded David, who was about to be captured; but a message arrived with news that the Philistines had invaded Israel, and the king had to break of his pursuit and go to fight the enemy. God protected and prospered David.

The Bible relates that on two occasions Saul was at the mercy of David, who refrained from attacking the king. Let's look at one of those incidents, which happened in the region of En Gedi. Here is the story:

Saul took three thousand chosen men from all Israel and set out to look for David and his men near the Crags of the Wild Goats. He came to the sheep pens along the way; a cave was there, and Saul went in to relieve himself. David and his men were far back in the cave. The men said, "This is the day the Lord spoke of when he said to you, 'I will give your enemy into your hands for you to deal with as you wish.'" Then David crept up unnoticed and cut off a corner of Saul's robe. Afterward, David was conscience-stricken for having cut off a corner of his robe. He said to his men, "The Lord forbid that I should do such a thing to my master, the Lord's anointed, or lift my hand against him; for he is the anointed of the Lord."[24]

Try to recreate that moment in your mind. Your worst enemy, who is pursuing you to kill you, falls into your hands. He is at your mercy. Your friends tell you that this is God's doing, fulfilling His promises to deliver your enemy to you. You are aware that the divine promises will be completely fulfilled only by the death of your enemy. If you kill him, the misery in which you are living will end and everything will change for the better. If you were in David's place, what would you do? David, by means of what we now call "the mind of Christ," was able to understand a spiritual reality that took precedence over the circumstances. He was able to see that it was not up to him to take God's time into his hands to speed up the fulfillment of His promises, and in spite of the pressures of the moment, he wisely chose to move within the framework of God's timing. And if this happened to you twice, would you act the same way both times? David did. When the king learned of David's action, he declared, *"You have just now told me of the good you did to me; the Lord delivered me into your hands, but you did not kill me. When a man finds his enemy, does he let him get away unharmed?...I know that you will surely be king and that the kingdom of Israel will be established in your hands."*[25]

In spite of all his promises, King Saul did not stop pursuing his son-in-law. David became tired of such a life and began to despair and lose confidence in God's protection, saying that sooner or later Saul would kill him. So he decided to leave Israel and go with his six hundred men to Philistia, the land of the arch-enemies of his people. This constituted a lack of faith in the Lord who had always protected him. Achish king of Gath received David warmly and allowed him to live in the city of Ziklag. David supported himself by raiding the neighboring areas outside of Philistia, and he killed everyone that he encountered in these raids to leave no witnesses, making sure that no one would tell the Philistine king. Meanwhile, David was lying to King Achish, leading him to believe that he was attacking territories of the Israelites. The cracks in David's character were becoming visible; and his actions are inexcusable, because he was lying, plundering, and killing with impunity. The Philistines began to prepare to attack Israel, and King Achish asked his vassal to fight with him against his own people. We do not know whether David really intended to do this, but he promised to accompany the Philistine army. The commanders of that army, however, did not trust David and demanded that Achish not allow him to go with them. They feared that in the battle this former champion of Israel would fight for his own people. What would have happened to David if he had fought on the side of the enemy, particularly in that battle in which King Saul and three of his sons were killed, including Jonathan? His history would have been different.

Upon the death of King Saul, David was proclaimed king in Hebron over the southern tribes led by Judah. At the same time a son of Saul named Ish-Bosheth was made king over the northern tribes, which called themselves Israel. This movement was led by Abner, Saul's general, who had not died in the battle. This division sparked a bloody civil war that continued for the two years of Ish-Bosheth's reign, until he was assassinated by his own people. General Abner, who had decided to unite with David, was also killed by Joab, David's general, in an act of personal vengeance. Faced by these events, the northern tribes decided to proclaim David their king. Thus David came to reign over the entire nation. The Scripture says, *"David was thirty years old when he became king, and he reigned forty years. In Hebron he reigned over Judah seven years and six months, and in Jerusalem he reigned over all Israel and Judah thirty-tree years."*[26] David waited between twelve and eighteen years to become king. And you, how long have you waited for a promise from God?

Jesus Christ: The Coming King

In Jesus Christ will be fulfilled all the Messianic promises given to David about a perpetual kingdom. This "Son of David" will establish His kingdom, not only over Israel but also over the entire world. The imminence of our Lord's return is a message that has been preached since the very beginning of the Church, and His return continues to be imminent. Christ is coming, and each day we do our part of hasten His return. Frequently we hear songs that speak of the Lord's delay in coming to receive His Church. One says, "Lord, delay no longer; send Jesus Christ to us now." In spite of the good intentions of these authors, the apostle Peter, speaking of the return of Christ, clearly says:

> But do not forget this one thing, dear friends: With the Lord a day is like a thousand years, and a thousand years are like a day. The Lord is not slow in keeping his promise, as some understand slowness. He is patient with you, not wanting anyone to perish, but everyone to come to repentance.[27]

The return of our Lord, and everything that will accompany it, is the great hope of the Church. In spite of the mocking the Church suffers because she awaits the return of her King, we know that His delay is due to God's prolonged mercy, which waits in order to add one more name to the list of those saved and liberated by Jesus Christ. Thank you, Lord, for waiting for me!

The exclamation which ends the Book of Revelation, *"Come, Lord Jesus!"*, is a missionary cry. That is to say, to declare, proclaim, and desire the return of Christ must be motivated by a genuine desire to meet our Savior. Therefore it should move us to testify about Jesus and to procure by all means that every people upon earth learn of the hope of eternal life which we have in Jesus Christ. We should not want the Lord to return to end our difficulties and tribulations. Let us not despair, but rather do our part to hasten

His coming, as we announce the imminent return of Jesus Christ, our Coming King.

When we choose to think and act according to the mind of Christ within us, we allow the Lord to lead us in the manner that He wishes. We approach the perfect will of God for the pilgrimage of our existence. It is not so much that we make desperate efforts to know what the Lord wants us to do, rather we make sure to maintain our communion with Him. Everything else will flow from that. Our experience along the way will help us to tune our ear to distinguish and follow the voice of God, which comes to us in a multitude of ways. The Holy Spirit wants to show the evidence, the fruit, or the results of His presence in us. As we allow Him to do this, we will be living in what Paul calls the mind of Christ. We will go forward, sowing our path with forgiveness, understanding, tolerance and love, particularly toward those who do nothing to deserve them.

As you begin each day, look at yourself in the mirror and say, "Lord, help me to live today thinking and acting controlled by the mind of Christ within me." Then go out to live life following the example of Jesus Christ, which, above all else, is striking and revolutionary.

Our life is like a bridge. Let us cross it without attempting to build a permanent home upon it. Let us pursue our heavenly home; here we are merely pilgrims and strangers. Let us not live as though this were our final destination. Our hope is something out of this world! Let us place our future in the warm, sure hands of our Teacher, convinced of His love and His power. There is no one like Him to guide us through the green prairies or in the deep, dark, and dangerous valleys, in quiet or in turbulent waters. Every difficulty will be used to conform us to His image. Only the person who walks hand-in-hand with the Good Shepherd can travel safely, for God has a marvelous plan for his life. Lord, grant us understanding beyond the merely human and ordinary!

His Plan for Me

When I appear before the Judgment Seat of Christ and He shows me the plan He had for my life, the plan for my life as it could have been if I had done His will; and when I see how I hindered Him here, and ran beyond Him there, and refused to surrender my will; there will be sadness in the eyes of my Savior, sadness, because He will still love me. He wanted me to be rich, but I will stand there poor, with absolutely nothing, only His grace, while my memory flees like a frightened thing though paths that I cannot walk again. Then my desolate heart will nearly break from tears which I cannot shed. I will cover my face with my empty hands, and bow my head which has no crown. Lord, the years which are left to me, I place them in your hands. Take me and mould me in order to fulfill the purpose which you have planned.[28]

Endnotes by Chapters

Endnotes—Chapter 1

[1] 1 Corinthians 2:9a
[2] 1 Corinthians 2:10
[3] Acts 20:35
[4] A.W. Tozer, *That Incredible Christian, 24*
[5] Luke 24:25
[6] John 6:6
[7] Luke 5:5
[8] Ezequiel 37:3
[9] Romans 12:2
[10] Isaiah 55:8-9
[11] John 15:15
[12] Setter, Hugo M. *Concordance of the Greek New Testament,*
[13] Proverbs 23:7 (NKJV)
[14] Colossians 1:21
[15] Romans 14:22
[16] Romans 12:2
[17] Matthew 15:19

Endnotes—Chapter 2

[1] 1 Corinthians 2:12
[2] Genesis 37:6-11
[3] Genesis 15:13

Dr. Daniel Villa

[4]Genesis 50:20
[5] Genesis 45:4-5, 7-8
[6]Romans 8:28
[7]2 Kings 5:11
[8] 2 Kings 5:10
[9] John 3:15
[10]Luke 24:20-21
[11]Isaiah 53:4-5
[12]2 Corinthians 12:10
[13]James 3:13-18
[14] Isaiah 43:1-2

Endnotes—Chapter 3

[1] Mark 3:17
[2]Luke 9:54
[3] Raymond L. Cramer, *The Psychology of Jesus and Mental Health*, p. 18
[4] Author unknown
[5] Acts 12:1-10
[6]2 Kings 6:16
[7]Psalm 23:1-4
[8] Jeremiah 1:8, 18-19
[9] Roberto C. Savage and José Andrade. *El Drama del Curaray, 16.*
[10] Quoted by William Barclay, *Commentary on the N.T.: Matthew, p*
[11]Elisabeth Elliot, *Through Gates of Splendor* (Pyramid Pub. for Fleming Revell, 1977) p. 204

Endnotes—Chapter 4

[1] 2 Corinthians 12:10b
[2]1 Samuel 17:5-7

[3] 1 Samuel 17:45
[4] 1 Samuel 17:8
[5] 1 Samuel 17:26b
[6] 1 Samuel 17:47
[7] Psalm 44:3
[8] *Hymns of the Christian Life* #356 (Christian Publications, Camp Hill, PA, 1978)
[9] Philippians 3:6-8
[10] Galatians 4:13-15; 6:11; Colossians 1:1; 4:18; 2 Thes. 1:1; 3:17; 1 Cor. 16:21
[11] Ezekiel 28:24; 2 Timothy 4:14-15
[12] 2 Corinthians 12:9a
[13] 2 Corinthians 12:9-10
[14] Lloyd J. Ogilvie, *Falling into Greatness* (Editorial Vida, Miami) 190
[15] Revelation 5:5
[16] Revelation 5:6
[17] Leighton Ford, *The Christian Persuader* (Harper & Row, New York, 1985) 154
[18] Author unknown

Endnotes—Chapter 5

[1] Louis Berkhof, *Sistematic Theology* (Eerdmans, Grand Rapids 1941) 48
[2] *Hymns of the Christian Life* #33 (Christian Publications, Camp Hill, PA, 1978)
[3] Job 37:22, 23
[4] J.I. Packer, *Knowing God* (1973) 73
[5] *Ibid.*
[6] Exodus 18:11

[7] Exodus 15:11

[8] Isaiah 40:12

[9] *Enciclopedia Hispana,* Tomo 9, 199.317

[10] *Ibid.* 318

[11] J. Roberto Spangler, *Dios en Primer Lugar* (Asociación Casa Editora Sudamericana, 1977) 31

[12] *Enciclopedia Hispana,* Tomo 10, 216

[13] *Ibid.,* Tomo 13, 233

[14] *Ibid.*

[15] *Enciclopedia Cumbre,* Tomo 14 (Editorial La Cumbre, 1983) 167

[16] *Ibid.* 271

[17] *Ibid.*

[18] Isaiah 40:16

[19] I Timothy 1:17

[20] Neil Anderson, *Rompiendo las Cadenas* (Editorial Unilit, 1998) 28

[21] Myer Perlman, *Teología Bíblica Sistemática,* (Editorial Vida, 1985) 83

[22] Genesis 3:5

[23] Matthew 4:9

[24] Billy Graham, *Angels: God's Secret Agents* (Word Publishing, 1986) 65

[25] *Frases Célebres y Citas* (Editorial Sopena, 1994) 442

[26] Richard J. Foster, *Dinero, Sexo y Poder* (Editorial Betania, 1989) 145

[27] *Frases Célebres y Citas*, 393

[28] Tom Eisenman, *Temptations Men Face,* (Intervarsity Press, 1990) 120, 121

[29] Mark 9:35

[30] Luke 9:48c

[31] *Frases Célebres y Citas,* 393

[32] Luke 14:8-11

[33] E.F. Harrison, *El Comentario Bíblico Moody* (Editorial Moody 1971) 121

[34] R. Jamieson, *Comentario Exegético y Explicativo de la Biblia,* Tomo II (Casa Bautista de Publicacions, 1977) 155

[35] *Frases Célebres y Citas,* 380

[36] Matthew 12:15-21; Luke 22:27

[37] Matthew 20:20-28

[38] G. Hendriksen, *El Evangelio Según San Mateo* (Subcomisión Literatura Cristiana, 1960) 785

Endnotes—Chapter 6

[1] Ecclesiastes 3:1

[2] 2 Peter 3:8

[3] Author unknown

[4] Galatians 4:4

[5] Genesis 15:3-4

[6] Genesis 12:4

[7] Genesis 16:1-5

[8] *Islam, un Llamado al Arrepentimiento* (Acción Misionera en Nicaragua) 10

[9] Genesis 17:5-21

[10] Genesis 46:26

[11] Exodus 1:7

[12] Acts 7:25

[13] Guthrie & Motyer, eds. *Nuevo Comentario Bíblico* (Casa Bautista de Publicaciones) 105

[14] Juan Bosch, David, *Biografía de un Rey ,* 13

[15] *Op. cit.* Juan Bosch, 65

[16] 1 Samuel 16:13
[17] 1 Samuel 18:7-9
[18] 1 Samuel 18:17
[19] 1 Samuel 18:25
[20] *Op. cit.* Juan Bosch, 95
[21] Richard Foster, *Dinero, Sexo y Poder* (Editorial Betania 1989) 145
[22] 1 Samuel 22:2
[23] 1 Samuel 23:17
[24] 1 Samuel 24:2-6
[25] 1 Samuel 24:18-20
[26] 2 Samuel 5:4-5
[27] 2 Peter 3:8-9
[28] Author unknown

BIBLIOGRAPHY

Anderson, Neil. *Rompiendo las cadenas.* Miami : Unilit, 1998.

Barclay, William. *Commentary on the N.T.: Matthew.* Barclay, Buenos Aires : Editorial la Aurora, 1973.

Berkhof, Louis. *Systematic Theology.* Grand Rapids : Eerdmans *Publishing,* 1941

Bosch, Juan. *David: biografía de un Rey.* Santo Domingo : Editorial Alfa y Omega, 1994.

Comentario bíblico Moody. Chicago : Editorial Moody, 1971.

Cramer, Raymond L. *The psychology of Jesus and mental health.* Grand Rapids : Zondervan Publishing House, 1959

Eisenman, Tom. *Temptations Men Face.* InterVarsity Press, 1990

Elliot, Elisabeth. *Through gates of splendor.* Old Tappan : Pyramid Publication by Fleming H. Revell, 1957.

Enciclopedia Hispánica. Barcelona : Encyclopedia Britannica Publishers, 1991.

Enciclopedia Ilustrada Cumbre. México : Editorial Cumbre, 1983.

Dr. Daniel Villa

Ford, Leighton. *The Christian Persuader.* New York: Harper & Row, 1985

Foster, Richard J. *Money, Sex and Power: The Challenge of the Disciplined Life.* Canada : HarperCollins, 1987

Graham, Billy. *Los Angeles, agentes secretos de Dios.* Miami : Editorial Caribe, 1989

Guthrie, D., J.A. Motyer, eds. *Nuevo comentario bíblico.* El Paso : Casa Bautista de Publicaciones, 1977.

Hendriksen, Guillermo. *El evangelio según San Mateo.* Grand Rapids : Subcomisión de Literatura Cristiana, 1986.

Hymns of the Christian Life #33. Camp Hill : Christian Publications, 1978

Islam, un llamado al arrepentimiento. Managua : Acción Misionera en Nicaragua.

Jamieson, Robert. *Comentario exegético y explicativo de la Biblia.* [El Paso] : Casa Bautista de Publicaciopnes, 1975.

Ogilvie, Lloyd John. *Falling into greatness.* Nashville : Thomas Nelson, 1984

Parker, James I. *Knowing God .* Downers Grove, IL: InterVarsity Press, 1973

Perlman, Myer. *Teología bíblica y sistemática.* Miami : Editorial Vida, 1985.

Savage, Roberto C., José Andrade. *El drama del Curaray.*

Spangles, J. Roberto. *Dios en primer lugar.* Buenos Aires : Editora Sudamericana

Setter, Hugo M. *Concordance of the Greek New Testament*

Tozer, A.W. *That Incredible Christian.* Harrisburg : Christian Publication, 1964.

Made in the USA
Middletown, DE
09 October 2016